Kermadec Is.
SOUTH PACIFIC OCEAN
Three Kings Is.
Auckland
NORTH ISLAND
TASMAN SEA
Wellington
SOUTH ISLAND
Christchurch
Chatham Is.
Dunedin
STEWART ISLAND
Bounty Is.
Snares Is.
Antipodes Is.
Auckland Is.
Campbell Is.
N
Farewell Spit
Stephens Island
Marlborough Sounds
Tasman Bay
Cook Strait
MARLBOROUGH
Seaward & Inland
Kaikoura Mountains
Kaikoura
TASMAN SEA
SOUTHERN ALPS
WESTLAND
Motunau Island
CANTERBURY
CHRISTCHURCH
Lake Ellesmere
Banks Peninsula
Lake Tekapo
MACKENZIE COUNTRY
Lake Hawea
FIORDLAND
Lake Hayes
OTAGO
Lake Wakatipu
PACIFIC OCEAN
Lake Te Anau
DUNEDIN
Taiaroa Head
Otago Peninsula
Lake Hauroko
SOUTHLAND
Catlins
N
Solander Is.
Foveaux Strait
Codfish Island
Stewart Island/Rakiura

Contents

Introduction	8
Huia	10

Forest and islands 12

Sweet-toothed birds
Tui	14
Bellbird	16
Stitchbird	18
New Zealand pigeon	20
Chatham Island pigeon	22
Kokako	24

Parrots
Kaka	26
Kakapo	28
Red-crowned parakeet	30
Antipodes Island parakeet	32
Orange-fronted parakeet	34

Insect eaters
Fantail	36
New Zealand robin	38
Black robin	40
Yellowhead	42
Rifleman	44
Shining cuckoo	46
Saddleback	48
Morepork	50
Brown kiwi	52
Little spotted kiwi	54
New Zealand snipe	56
Weka	58

High country 60

Falcon	62
Kea	64
Rock wren	66
Takahe	68

Town and country 70

Out the window
Blackbird	72
Song thrush	74
Starling	76
Grey warbler	78
Silvereye	80
House sparrow	82
Hedge sparrow	84
Goldfinch	86
Greenfinch	88
Chaffinch	90

Open country
Skylark	92
Yellowhammer	94
Cirl bunting	96
Redpoll	98
Spur-winged plover	100
Australian magpie	102
Australasian harrier	104
Little owl	106
Sacred kingfisher	108
Pheasant	110
Peafowl	112
Turkey	114

For Hirini — Mou te tai ata, moku te tai po (*RM*)

For Claire and Todd, with love (*AB*)

Be Like The Bird

Be like the bird, who
Resting in his flight
On a twig too slight
Feels it bend beneath him,
Yet sings
Knowing he has wings.

Victor Hugo

Helmeted guineafowl	116
California quail	118
Bobwhite quail	120
Brown quail	122

Wetlands and rivers 124

Wrybill	126
Black stilt	128
Black-fronted tern	130
Mallard duck	132
Grey duck	134
Blue duck	136
Canada goose	138
Paradise shelduck	140
White-faced heron	142
Mute swan	144
Black swan	146
Pukeko	148
Banded rail	150
Australian coot	152
Fernbird	154

Sea and shore 156

Southern seas

Wandering albatross	158
Royal albatross	160
Campbell mollymawk	162
White-capped mollymawk	164
Salvin's mollymawk	166
Giant petrel	168
Brown skua	170
Chatham Island shag	172

Mainland seabirds

Red-billed gull	174
Black-backed gull	176
Caspian tern	178
Australasian gannet	180
Hutton's shearwater	182
Mottled petrel	184
Diving petrel	186
Fairy prion	188
Spotted shag	190
Bar-tailed godwit	192

Flightless seabirds

Campbell Island teal	194
Fiordland crested penguin	196
Snares crested penguin	198
Yellow-eyed penguin	200
Little blue penguin	202

Tropical waters

Red-tailed tropicbird	204
Wedge-tailed shearwater	206
White-naped petrel	208
Kermadec petrel	210
Tasman booby	212
Grey ternlet	214
White tern	216
Black noddy	218

Glossary	220
More information	222
Index	223

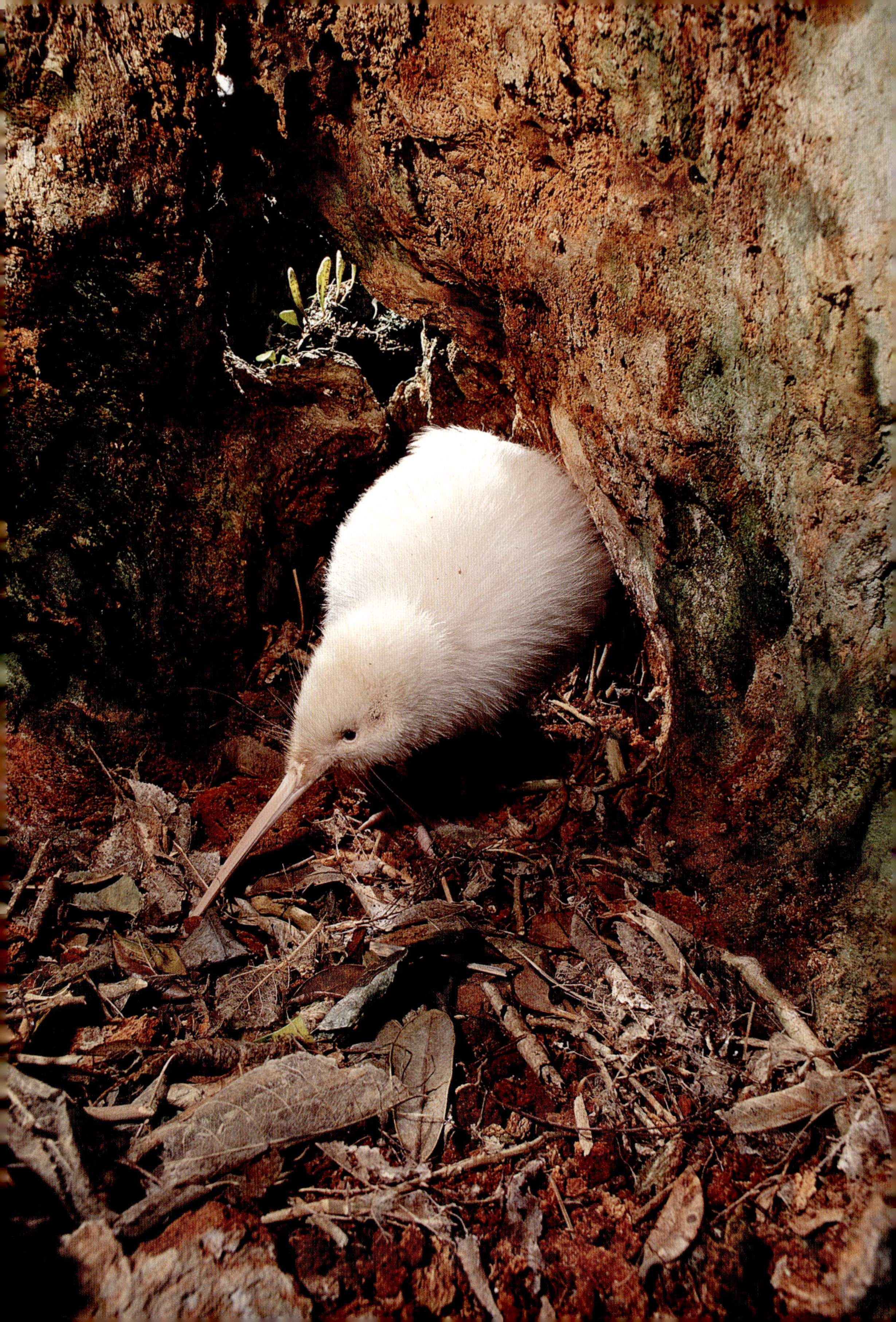

INTRODUCTION

Beautiful Birds of New Zealand is a celebration of beauty and diversity. It contains a very personal selection of a hundred birds from among the more than three hundred species that occur in the New Zealand region.

New Zealand is an ecologically diverse country, stretching across 22 degrees of latitude from the subtropical Kermadec Islands to subantarctic Campbell Island in the south. Its bird fauna is an interesting reflection of both its geographic location and its evolutionary and human history.

Surrounded by thousands of kilometres of ocean, the more than seven hundred islands in the New Zealand archipelago are important breeding grounds for seabirds ranging in size from tiny terns to the great albatrosses. Wading birds such as godwits make astonishing migrations to spend the southern summer on its long, rich shorelines. Isolated from other landmasses for tens of millions of years, New Zealand's land birds — such as the endemic kiwi, wrens and wattlebirds — are small in numbers but significant in their uniqueness.

Over the past two hundred years, European settlers have introduced many new bird species, with their motivations ranging from the aesthetic, in the case of the goldfinch, to the practical, in the case of pheasants and turkeys. The clearance of native forest by both Maori and Europeans, and the development of agriculture, also created opportunities for self-introduced birds such as spur-winged plovers.

The eclectic selection of birds in this book includes the unusual as well as the familiar, birds from the suburbs alongside species found only on remote islands, and rare endemic species as well as naturalised game birds. We have ordered our birds by habitat and ecological role, rather than the more traditional taxonomic checklist approach. (Be aware that bird taxonomy is in a state of flux, with some groups likely to be significantly rearranged in the near future.) There is a glossary on page 220.

While peacocks and tui are obvious candidates for a book on beautiful birds, we had no hesitation including giant petrels and starlings, as we believe beauty is about more than just appearance. Birdsong, courtship displays, intricately made nests and ecological significance are all part of what makes each bird such a wonderful treasure. In a book such as this we can barely begin to tell you each bird's story, so if you feel inspired to find out more, we have included lists of books and places where you can continue your own journey of discovery (page 221).

HUIA
Heteralocha acutirostris

The extinction of the huia is one of New Zealand's great tragedies. Revered by Maori and renowned among both fashionable and scientific Victorians, the huia was one of our most beautiful and unusual birds. Yet habitat destruction, voracious introduced predators and human greed sealed its fate before anyone realised it was doomed.

The huia was named by Maori for the sound of its loud distress call, a smooth unslurred whistling that sounded like *who-are-you-u*. A member of the New Zealand wattlebird family, this crow-like songbird is believed to be a very ancient part of the New Zealand avifauna. Like the related saddlebacks and kokako, huia had orange, fleshy wattles at the base of their bill, long strong legs for swinging and bounding through the forest, and were poor fliers.

The most outstanding feature of the species, however, was the marked sexual dimorphism of their bills — the most divergent of any bird species in the world. The female huia had a long, downward-curving bill, which she used as pliable forceps to penetrate the long holes made by the larvae of wood-boring beetles. The male, however, had a shorter bill, similar in shape to that of a saddleback; woodpecker-like, he inserted this short, powerful bill into bark or rotten wood, then opened it against the resistance of the wood to find prey. With their different bills serving different feeding functions, and the belief that pairs of birds worked together to find prey, huia are sometimes cited as an example of co-operative feeding. However, nineteenth-century naturalist Walter Buller, who often watched them feeding, stated that they didn't co-operate, so it's more likely that the different sexes made use of differing microhabitats.

Ironically, Buller played a large role in the demise of the huia. Having identified it as a natural wonder, he was one of a number of collectors who harvested huia in large numbers for overseas museums and collectors. In 1883, Buller recorded how one party of eleven hunters in the Manawatu collected 646 huia skins in a single month. The huia became formally protected in 1892, and islands such as Kapiti and Little Barrier were being designated as sanctuaries specifically to protect them. But although Buller expressed support for such moves, instead of catching birds for release on the islands he continued to shoot them 'in the interests of science'. In 1893, Buller captured a pair of huia, but rather than transfer them to an island sanctuary he took them to England.

Pre-European Maori held the huia to be one of their most beautiful and sacred

1

birds, and only high-ranking chiefs and their families could wear its white-tipped black tail feathers in their hair. In 1901, a high-ranking Maori woman took a huia feather from her hair and put it in the Duke of York's hat-band as a sign of esteem and respect. This simple act reduced huia from sacred treasure to European fashion accessory, helping seal a fate already set in motion by forest clearance, scientific collectors and introduced cats, stoats and rats.

The last huia officially seen alive were two males and one female, recorded on December 28, 1907. The extinction of this extraordinary species did at least mark a turning point in European attitudes to native species, and an end to the rampant imperialistic views of naturalists such as Buller. Soon after the huia's extinction the Forestry League and the New Zealand Forest and Bird Protection Society were established, and New Zealanders began to consider their responsibility for protecting unique, beautiful birds.

A hundred or so years later we have, as a nation, matured. We have stopped public logging of native forests, and are tackling the enormous problem of introduced predators. Although we haven't been able to stop the extinction of several other species of wonderful endemic birds, we are doing our best to save those that are left, including the huia's extraordinary relatives — the gregarious saddleback and the glorious songster, the kokako.

Forest and islands

Tui have a notch in the eighth primary feather of each wing, which creates a distinctive noise when they fly. This noise is particularly noticeable in male birds.

TUI
Prosthemadera novaeseelandiae

Tui are the largest and boldest of the New Zealand honeyeaters. Unquestionably one of this country's most familiar and iconic native birds, they were recently voted New Zealand's inaugural 'bird of the year'. The collective noun for tui is the delightful 'ecstasy of tui'.

Honeyeaters are the most successful passerine family in Australasia, with 177 species scattered throughout Australia, New Guinea, Indonesia, Hawaii and the southwest Pacific. Only a few honeyeaters, including the Hawaiian ones, are as large and strikingly marked as the tui. Honeyeaters are important pollinators of flowers, and have a long, protrusive tongue with a brush-like tip for extracting nectar.

In New Zealand, tui belong to an ecological guild of nectar-feeders that includes bellbirds, stitchbirds, kaka and, more recently, silvereyes. Of these birds, tui are the most vigorously aggressive, displaying and threatening others over shared feeding resources such as flowering pohutukawa. However, when nectar levels are at their highest they may only defend part of a tree, so smaller birds are still able to feed.

Tui have strong legs and sharp claws that enable them to clamber adroitly around flowers and foliage as they feed, even hanging upside down. They exploit the regular flowering patterns of trees in both native forest and in suburbia, where kowhai, flowering eucalypts and banksias are good nectar sources. They may have a feeding range of up to 100 kilometres, enabling them to move seasonally between food sources.

As well as nectar, tui eat a large number of invertebrates such as stick insects, cicadas and dragonflies, especially when they are feeding chicks. They also play an important ecological role in distributing medium-sized seeds of forest trees. Tui establish breeding territories in spring by singing from high perches in the early morning and late evening; rich, melodious notes are intermingled with clicks, coughs, croaks and grunts, especially in younger birds. Tui dialects vary between areas.

A subspecies of tui found on the Chatham Islands is one-fifth larger and heavier than mainland tui, with longer white throat tufts. The only honeyeater remaining on the Chatham Islands, this subspecies has almost disappeared on the main island, and there may be fewer than 500 birds remaining, mostly on South East Island, with some on Pitt Island.

SWEET-TOOTHED BIRDS

🕊 *Joseph Banks, naturalist on board Captain Cook's* Endeavour, *was woken by a dawn chorus of bellbirds in Queen Charlotte Sound in 1770. He described the sound as 'almost imitating small bells but with the most tuneable silver sound imaginable'.*

BELLBIRD
Korimako *Anthornis melanura*

Bellbirds are typical Australasian honeyeaters; medium-sized forest birds with dull green plumage. But unlike many honeyeaters that have specialised pollinating relationships with particular plant species, bellbirds are generalists that pollinate a range of flowers.

Bird-pollinated flowers are typically red or yellow and rich in nectar and pollen, with several distinctive types of flowers. Pohutukawa, rata and *Xeronema*, or Poor Knights lily, clump hundreds of flowers into brush-like clusters. Kowhai, flax, rewarewa and fuchsia have long, narrow, tubular flowers. Red mistletoes have the most specialised relationship with the honeyeaters, relying on bellbirds and tui to tweak the tips of the closed buds, which then burst open explosively. As bellbirds forage for nectar, yellow, orange or even blue pollen, in the case of fuchsia, is liberally deposited on their foreheads, chins, cheeks and chests, and transferred between flowers. At any one time a bellbird may be carrying thousands of pollen grains, from several different plant species, in its feathers.

In South Island beech forests, bellbirds obtain much of their sugar from honeydew secreted by beech scale insects, but they now face severe competition for this food supply from introduced European wasps. In late summer, when flowers are uncommon, bellbirds eat fruit, glean for spiders and insects on tree trunks and leaves, and hawk for small flying insects.

Once widespread throughout New Zealand, bellbirds swiftly and mysteriously disappeared from north of the Waikato during the 1860s, although they remained on nearby offshore islands, and survived elsewhere on the mainland in the presence of introduced mammalian predators. The endemic bellbird occurs as far south as the Auckland Islands, with a subspecies found on the Three Kings Islands to the north and another on the Poor Knights Islands. The large, robust Chatham Island bellbird, almost the size of the mainland tui, became extinct during the 1860s.

Pairs of bellbirds keep the same breeding territory from year to year, and may raise two broods of chicks in a breeding season. Up to five pinkish-white eggs, with pink-brown spots, are laid in the feather-lined cup of a rather untidy nest of sticks and twigs. On offshore islands, bellbirds shelter their nests in rock crevices, deep-forking branches or under flax bushes, to avoid damage from seabirds crashing through the forest canopy.

SWEET-TOOTHED BIRDS

Stitchbirds, or hihi, are strongly sexually dimorphic: males have a black head and distinctive yellow and white markings, while the females are drab brown. Both sexes have flycatcher-like bristles on their faces.

STITCHBIRD
Hihi *Notiomystis cincta*

Stitchbirds have always been classified as honeyeaters, but recent DNA analysis has revealed they are in fact a unique and ancient bird group whose nearest relatives appear to be New Zealand wattlebirds such as kokako. This revelation explains why stitchbirds, or hihi, have always been such an anomaly amongst the honeyeaters.

Stitchbirds are highly sociable birds, at the bottom of the nectar-feeding pecking order. They have a remarkable, flexible breeding system; depending on availability of food and nesting holes they might be monogamous, or they may have several mates, or even be a group of several females and males breeding together. This latter strategy is very rare amongst passerines, with only a small handful of other species mating this way. Stitchbirds are also highly unusual in the bird world for using a range of mating positions, including face-to-face copulation on the forest floor (which is considered a forced mating).

Stitchbirds nest in holes in trees, and build a complex nest above the cavity entrance. The female wrestles rigid sticks into the cavity to build a firm base, then weaves a nest of finer materials on top. Females carry out all the incubating and most of the chick-feeding duties. Males defend an area of forest around the nest during the ten or so days the female is fertile, and then look for other mating opportunities; nearly 90 percent of hihi nests have chicks from more than one father.

After leaving parental care youngsters flock together and are regularly babysat by an adult male. These juvenile groups remain loosely together during their first winter. Stitchbird fledglings play games, such as two birds pushing each other along a branch until one bird falls and hangs upside down while the other perches above. They also play follow-the-leader, with one bird entering all sorts of cavities to collect insects and spiderwebs while two or three others follow.

Named for their *stitch*-like call, stitchbirds were common throughout the North Island until European settlement. By 1883, however, they were extinct everywhere except Little Barrier Island, where they survived in the presence of cats and kiore. The species has thrived since these predators were eradicated, and birds have been successfully transferred to sanctuaries on Tiritiri Matangi, Kapiti and Mokoia islands.

New Zealand pigeons are such important seed-dispersers that they are considered to have been a major force in the rapid expansion of podocarp forests following the last major glaciation, around 14,000 years ago.

NEW ZEALAND PIGEON

Kereru, Kuka, Kukupa *Hemiphaga novaeseelandiae*

Of the world's fruit-eating pigeons the New Zealand pigeon is the most handsome, both in size and colour. They play an important ecological role in New Zealand forests, dispersing large seeds.

Although New Zealand pigeons, also known variously as wood pigeons, kereru, kuka or kukupa, are still widespread on New Zealand's three main islands and many offshore islands, fossil evidence shows they used to be much more abundant. Even today these pigeons reach high numbers in podocarp forest dominated by rimu trees, feeding extensively on rimu fruit and spreading its seeds. Before deforestation their preferred forests were matai; matai are the richest-fruiting podocarp, and such forest typically also had an abundance of seasonal resources such as the leaves and flowers of kowhai, wineberry and lacebark.

Fossil deposits reveal that New Zealand pigeons were common prey for the now extinct Eyles's harrier and laughing owl, as well as the falcon. From the earliest settlement they were also a favoured food for Maori, as their tameness and noisy, cumbersome flight made them easy to hunt.

When not feeding New Zealand pigeons rest on branches, with their drooping tails half opened, wings closely folded and their heads tucked in; their large white breasts are very conspicuous. During the breeding season birds of both sexes fly swiftly upwards, stall, then dive steeply on folded wings back to the trees. The male may also puff up his neck feathers and bounce up and down on the spot next to the female, calling gently.

Their nest is a flimsy flat twiggy platform, often so thin that the single white egg can be seen from underneath. But despite the casual appearance of the nest the birds are attentive parents, both brooding and feeding their chick rich pigeon milk produced from the wall of the crop. When the chick is larger it's fed a pulp of regurgitated fruit.

Numbers of New Zealand pigeons declined following Maori settlement due to the clearance of lowland forest by fire, and again following European settlement when they were hunted with firearms. Today, possums are a major threat, both as predator and competitor: they are large enough to push a bird off the nest at night before eating eggs or chicks, and they compete with pigeons for other food.

The Chatham Island pigeon is one of a large number of threatened pigeon species worldwide. As unlikely as it might seem, the world's most famous extinct bird, the flightless dodo, was also a pigeon.

CHATHAM ISLAND PIGEON
Parea *Hemiphaga chathamensis*

The Chatham Island pigeon or parea, long regarded as a subspecies of the New Zealand pigeon, is nearly twenty percent heavier than its mainland relative, making it one of the world's largest pigeons.

The Chatham Island pigeon has a small head and large, full body. Its striking white chest-straps and belly are similar to those of the New Zealand pigeon, but its more robust two-toned bill is red with an orange tip, and its plumage is purple and grey, rather than green and red-brown. These pigeons were once widespread and common on all the main islands of the Chathams group — so much so that their bones are the most abundant found in fossil middens.

Large-scale forest clearance following European settlement in the early 1800s, further forest degradation by sheep and cattle, and predation by introduced cats, rats and later possums, caused a rapid decline in many Chatham birds, including the pigeon. By 1990, just 40 or so pigeons survived. Habitat protection and predator control in some areas have seen numbers increase to between 150 and 200 birds, but they continue to decline in unprotected areas. They are found today mainly in the last extensive areas of forest in the south of the main island, with six or so birds on Pitt Island, and possibly two surviving on South East Island following a translocation in the 1980s.

On the Chatham Islands, forest has a much simpler structure than on mainland New Zealand, with four species of canopy tree which seldom reach more than 10 metres in height. Several broadleaf tree species rely solely on the parea for seed dispersal, and the hoho, or Chatham Island lancewood, is the most important species for the pigeon. Hoho is found in most forests, especially in coastal forest in damp gullies and moist gentle slopes, but it is also eaten by cattle and possums.

Although they usually breed in winter and spring when their main food is available, Chatham Island pigeons can breed year-round if it is a good hoho fruiting year. They spend much time on the forest floor, feeding and courting, as did the now-extinct Chatham Island kaka.

SWEET-TOOTHED BIRDS

While North Island kokako have disc-shaped cobalt-blue wattles, the rest of the wattlebird family have orange wattles.

KOKAKO
Callaeas wilsoni

Kokako belong to the endemic New Zealand wattlebird family, a very ancient bird family with no close relatives. The family includes the North Island and South Island kokako, saddlebacks and the extinct huia, all defined by fleshy wattles at the gape of their jaw, long legs and weak flight.

Kokako rely on rich, undisturbed, old-growth forest with an abundance of different plants flowering and fruiting throughout the year. They inhabit all levels of the forest from the canopy down to the forest floor, and progress through the trees much like a flying squirrel. They bound and jump up through different levels to the canopy on their long, well-developed legs, and glide down or flutter heavily from tree to tree using their small wings. Kokako feed in the canopy, in the understorey or on the forest floor during the day.

Kokako form lifelong pairs, and mutually defend permanent territories. At dawn they sing from the tallest trees in their territory, and they are renowned for their beautiful, complex, haunting song with its final melancholy note. This song, heard by conservationists among the impressive, column-like trunks of Pureora's podocarp trees in the late 1970s, precipitated a turning point in conservation history in New Zealand. It was the first time a majority of New Zealanders realised how many native species were being lost, including secretive forest birds such as the kokako, and it led to a widespread call for a halt to native logging.

Once widespread in the North Island, the North Island kokako is now restricted to about fifteen scattered locations, with most of these populations in decline due to poor nesting success and predation of nesting females. As well as foraging on the ground, kokako usually nest close to tree trunks, which makes eggs, chicks and even adults highly susceptible to predation by cats, rats, possums and stoats. Although intensive management has stabilised a few of these populations, the only safe populations are those on predator-free offshore islands.

South Island kokako were once found throughout the South Island and Stewart Island, but are now considered extinct, although some ornithologists believe a few individuals survive in several remote locations.

Like most largely vegetarian parrots, kaka eat many parts of plants including fruit, seeds and buds.

KAKA
Nestor meridionalis

Parrots are usually brightly coloured and noisy — a description that applies well to the introduced Australian parrots that now breed here, but kaka and the eight other species of parrots and parakeets native to New Zealand are quite different.

Worldwide there are more than 350 species of parrots, widely spread across lowland tropical and subtropical forests in Central and South America, Africa, Madagascar, South-East Asia, Australasia and Polynesia. Compared to New Zealand's eccentric nocturnal flightless kakapo (see page 28) and the omnivorous kea (see page 64), which hunts and kills other birds, the endemic kaka may seem a little ordinary, but in fact they are remarkable birds.

They are the largest member of our native forests' nectar-feeding guild, foraging for nectar on pohutukawa, rata and mistletoe flowers. Kaka also attack the bark and wood of pohutukawa and rata, making horizontal cuts with their bills that cause the sweet sap to run.

Kaka fill the ecological niche of woodpeckers; interestingly, there are no true woodpeckers in New Zealand's podocarp forests, New Guinea's oak forests or Australia's eucalypt forests. Kaka feed on the large larvae of wood-boring beetles in rotten wood. These are such an important source of protein and fats that a kaka may devote more than an hour to extracting one larva. Kaka have traditionally been able to compensate for the energy used finding larvae by feeding on sugar-rich honeydew on beech tree trunks. However, competition with introduced wasps for this food resource is just one of a number of factors that have contributed to a major decline in kaka numbers in both the North and South islands, although they still occur in reasonable numbers on islands such as Stewart Island, Kapiti and Little Barrier.

The decline in mistletoe caused by possums has also affected kaka numbers, and stoat predation has had a severe impact on females and chicks, which are particularly vulnerable as it is difficult for them to escape from the nest cavity when threatened. The Chatham Island kaka, which became extinct after the arrival of Europeans, had very robust legs compared to mainland kaka, and although it could fly it was essentially a ground-dwelling bird.

Kakapo have typical parrot feet, with the outer two toes pointing backwards and gripping in opposition to the two forward-pointing toes. This strong grasp enables them to climb well, and gives them a distinctive rolling gait.

KAKAPO
Strigops habroptilus

Flightless kakapo are not only one of the world's most unusual parrots, and the largest by weight; they are also one of its rarest. Their mottled, moss-green plumage and nocturnal habits once served them well, protecting them from the now-extinct Eyles's harrier and giant eagle.

Kakapo were numerous in both the North and South islands, although curiously no fossils have ever been found on Stewart Island. But everything changed with the arrival of humans and mammalian predators, and by the 1970s only a handful of male birds, in Fiordland, were known to exist. In 1977 a small population was discovered on Stewart Island, and during the 1980s as many birds as possible were transferred to predator-free offshore islands, a move which certainly saved the species from extinction. The kakapo is now considered extinct in its former natural range.

Most parrots are monogamous, but kakapo are a notable exception. Unusually for parrots — and for New Zealand birds — they have a lek mating system. Males gather at night in a display ground, or lek, and advertise their presence with loud, booming calls. Females visit these sites and mate with the male of their choice, after which they raise the chicks on their own. Kakapo breed infrequently — every two to five years — timing their breeding with the occasional mast-fruiting of podocarp trees such as rimu. Kakapo breed very late in the season, with the female rearing the chicks through winter, when the rimu fruit ripens.

Intensive management, including hand-rearing and the use of supplementary feeding (initially to try to induce breeding and more recently to ensure a reliable food supply for females with chicks) has seen kakapo numbers increase from a low of 51 birds to 86 birds in 2006. Kakapo are long-lived birds, and recent breeding successes have changed the population from one dominated by aging male birds to one with many young females. However, it will be many years before the population will be large enough for the species to survive without human intervention.

On islands with limited fresh water, red-crowned parakeets regularly visit springs and seepages to drink.

RED-CROWNED PARAKEET
Kakariki *Cyanoramphus novaezelandiae*

Cyanoramphus parakeets were widespread in the South Pacific, from New Caledonia to Tahiti, until human colonisation resulted in the loss of all the populations in eastern Polynesia. The most widespread of the New Zealand *Cyanoramphus* group were the red-crowned parakeets or kakariki, which occurred from the subtropical Lord Howe and Kermadec islands to the subantarctic Macquarie, Auckland and Antipodes islands.

Once extremely abundant on the main islands of New Zealand, from the coast up to the mountains, red-crowned parakeet species are now rare on the mainland and extinct on Campbell, Macquarie and Lord Howe islands, although still present in good numbers on the Auckland Islands and many small islands. Red-crowned parakeets spend much time foraging on the ground, a habit which partially explains why they have disappeared in the presence of introduced mammalian predators, yet survive on mammal-free offshore islands. Like the smaller yellow-crowned parakeets, which are still widespread on the mainland, red-crowned parakeets nest in holes, but their larger nest-holes may afford stoats and rats easier access.

They favour open scrubby areas rather than forest, and feed mostly on vegetable matter including berries, seeds, leaves, buds, shoots and even the aerial roots of pohutukawa trees. On the ground they scratch through leaf litter with a sideways movement of their feet. Their green plumage camouflages them as they feed in high foliage, when only their clicking bills and a steady stream of discarded food fragments falling to the ground gives them away. They are also insectivorous, eating scale insects and other forest plant pests, and if the opportunity arises they will eat meat, fat and eggs from penguin colonies. Fossil evidence shows they were in turn a common and important prey item for laughing owls and falcons.

When flying and when alarmed they give a prolonged, chattering *kek-kek-kek* call. Red-crowned parakeet pairs remain together year-round. Although they usually occur as pairs or in family groups, they were recorded in huge flocks in Marlborough and Canterbury in the 1880s. Outside the breeding season, on Mangere Island in the Chathams and Macauley Island in the Kermadecs, they still occur in large feeding groups in open grassland.

Like many island species, Antipodes Island parakeets are fearless and inquisitive. They seem attracted to the campsites of occasional visiting scientific parties, pecking at tent seams and pulling guy ropes.

ANTIPODES ISLAND PARAKEET
Cyanoramphus unicolor

While some outlying *Cyanoramphus* parakeet populations in the Pacific, such as the black-fronted and Society parakeets, were distinctively coloured, the New Zealand species are very similar to each other, both genetically and in looks. The plainest of them is the Antipodes Island or unicolour parakeet, a plump green bird with a swollen bulbous beak once described as an 'influenza-type nose'.

Endemic to the Antipodes Island group, this parakeet shares these treeless islands with a smaller and more widespread subantarctic red-crowned parakeet, called Reischek's parakeet. The main island is just 2025 hectares, but the two species have effectively divided the small island's habitats between them so there is no competition. Reischek's parakeets prefer the high, open central plateau and areas of short coastal tussock, while Antipodes Island parakeets are more common on steeper coastal slopes among tall, thick *Poa* tussock which may reach 2 metres in height, or along water courses in thickets of *Coprosma* and prickly shield fern.

They feed by walking over or climbing through tussock, biting off 20 centimetre lengths of *Poa* or *Carex* leaves which they hold in one foot. They progressively chew towards the tip, which they discard in characteristic piles. They have been known to scavenge penguin carcasses, and they have recently been observed digging storm petrel chicks out of their burrows and eating them; the fat may help them survive in the cold subantarctic climate.

In the absence of trees, the Antipodes parakeets nest in burrows, up to a metre long, in well-drained peat or in the base of tussocks or ferns. These are often abandoned seabird burrows, although the parakeets may dig their own. Reischek's parakeets, on the other hand, nest in the crowns of tussocks and ferns.

When alarmed, Antipodes Island parakeets make one or two deep, bubbling *kok-kok-kok* calls, before disappearing furtively into dense tussock. Reischek's parakeets tend to fly off in groups, chattering loudly.

Despite being largely terrestrial, Antipodes Island parakeets are strong fliers and on rare calm days both parakeet species can be seen swooping over the island's slopes, about 30 metres above the ground.

🕊 *Once recorded from sea level to the subalpine zone, orange-fronted parakeets are now found only in mountain beech forest where they eat scale insects and the flowers, leaves, buds and especially seeds of beech trees.*

ORANGE-FRONTED PARAKEET
Cyanoramphus malherbi

The orange-fronted parakeet was finally recognised as a species in 2000, yet this recognition may have come too late to save it. In that year an estimated seven to eight hundred birds were thought to survive; now, between just eighty and two hundred birds remain.

During the twentieth century the orange-fronted parakeet was considered a localised colour-variant of the yellow-crowned parakeet. Yet, as early as 1873, naturalist and collector Walter Buller had examined more than twenty individuals and concluded it was a separate species. Compared to the yellow-crowned parakeet, he described it as having a smaller and narrower bill; being a cold, pure green rather than a yellowish, grassy green; having an orange frontal band and a pale yellow crown; and living in an alpine habitat between 2000 and 2500 metres altitude.

In the 1880s orange-fronted parakeets were found throughout the South Island, on Stewart Island and on a few northern offshore islands, and in the 1890s they were said to be the dominant parakeet in some areas. Today they occur in just three valleys in North Canterbury: a small population in the Hawden, a significant population in the South Branch of the Hurunui, and a recently discovered population in the Poulter Valley.

Orange-fronted parakeets are hole-nesting birds that usually breed in summer, but during a mast year when beech trees produce enormous crops of seeds they may breed into the winter. Unfortunately the bumper seed-crops of beech-mast years also fuel population explosions of rats and stoats, and the hole-nesting, ground-feeding parakeet is easy prey for these predators.

In 2001 alone, rats were responsible for the loss of more than 600 orange-fronted parakeets in the Hurunui Valley. In that year an immediate response by the Department of Conservation to trap predators prevented the total extinction of the species. Ongoing predator-control programmes and captive breeding of birds for release on Chalky Island in Fiordland are slowing the decline, but lack of funding and basic knowledge continues to threaten New Zealand's 'newest' bird species.

Fantails are one of the few native species to have benefited from bush clearance and the subsequent creation of forest edge and scrub habitat.

FANTAIL
Piwakawaka *Rhipidura fuliginosa*

Fantails are one of our most common native birds, loved for their flamboyant tails, acrobatic flight and inquisitive friendliness. Yet, truth be told, their apparent love of human company is more a desire to befriend anything that disturbs or attracts insects.

New Zealand fantails are also found on Lord Howe and Norfolk islands. The closely related grey fantail occurs in mainland Australia and Tasmania. Members of the monarch flycatcher family, our fantails are browner on the body and whiter in the tail than other species. In the North Island fantails are typically pied, with a buff chest and a black-and-white tail; in the South Island nearly an eighth of fantails are pure black, with a white speck behind each eye.

Fantails are almost constantly in action, as with drooping wings and broadly fanned tails they flutter amid foliage to startle insects which they chase and catch in the air. The bristles around the gape of the bill act as a scoop, funnelling in insects. Tiny insects are caught and swallowed directly. Fantails may also catch larger flying insects, such as bluebottle flies, which they transfer from the beak to the foot and carry back to a branch. Then they grip their prey in their bills and beat it against the branch to kill it, before eating it.

Although they are usually aerial hunters, fantails will also search in crevices in bark, forage upside down on the underside of tree-fern fronds for moths hiding during the day, fossick in leaf litter on the ground, and even occasionally eat fruit.

Fantails are prolific breeders, and may produce up to five clutches in one season. Chicks leave the nest fourteen days after hatching and are fed by the male parent while the female builds the next nest. Built on a slender branch or fork in a tree, the nest is a neat cup of fine, dried grass, bark and moss, bound together with cobwebs and, in classic flycatcher style, is often protected by overhanging foliage.

In summer fantails occur alone or in pairs, but in winter they form loose flocks in warm, sheltered valleys or close to water. Bad winter weather or spring storms that affect their ability to find insects may cause sudden population crashes.

The male robin feeds his mate while she incubates their one to four eggs for eighteen days, calling her off the nest to feed every twenty minutes or so.

NEW ZEALAND ROBIN
Toutouwai *Petroica australis*

New Zealand bush robins display the same extraordinary tameness that endears the English robin to gardeners in the United Kingdom, but they don't belong to the same group as the true robins of America and Europe, which are actually related to thrushes. Our robins are members of the *Petroica* group of robin-like forest birds found in Australasia and New Guinea.

In an example of convergent evolution that further strengthens similarities with English robins, several of the Australian robins sport flame-red or pink breasts. The endemic New Zealand robin, however, is a drab, nondescript bird, grey above and cream below. Much larger than the Australian species, our robin has a more upright stance; longer, more slender legs; and spends much more time foraging on the ground.

New Zealand robins are perch-and-pounce hunters that will often stand motionless on a branch or log before jumping down onto the ground to snatch at invertebrate prey such as earthworms, spiders, amphipods, beetles, moths, caterpillars and weta. They also rummage through leaf litter, sometimes trembling one foot to encourage prey to move and give itself away.

While some populations of robins are shy, others endear themselves to trampers and campers by hopping right up to them, seeking titbits of food and searching nearby for insects disturbed by the presence of people.

The three subspecies of New Zealand robin occur in the North Island, South Island and Stewart Island, in native beech and podocarp forests, manuka and kanuka scrub and in some pine plantations. Since European settlement their numbers and distribution have declined significantly as a result of lowland forest clearance and introduced predators such as rats and stoats. Possums may also be affecting them by altering their habitats; after the eradication of possums on Kapiti Island, robin numbers increased dramatically.

Robins remain territorial year-round, especially during the breeding season between August and December, when the male patrols the territory and sings from prominent perches. His song is a loud, clear, musical trilling of descending notes. He also makes a quieter scolding chatter near the nest.

INSECT EATERS

Down to just five birds in the 1970s, there are now around 200 black robins. Efforts have begun to re-establish them on larger islands in the Chatham group, such as Pitt Island.

BLACK ROBIN
Toutouwai pango *Petroica traversi*

Australasian robins occur on islands from the subtropics to the subantarctic. While some species are generalists, with a widespread distribution across many islands in the western Pacific, other species such as the Chatham Island black robin have a very localised distribution.

Black robins are smaller and blacker than New Zealand robins (see page 38). They were once common on all the Chatham Islands, but introduced predators such as rats and cats soon caused a significant decline in numbers so that by 1976 only seven individuals remained, on Little Mangere Island. The black robin had the dubious distinction of being the rarest bird in the world for which the entire population was known.

In 1979, in response to a deteriorating habitat on Little Mangere Island, the entire population was moved to nearby Mangere Island, where the population fell still further, to just three males and two females. Only one of those females produced fertile eggs, so every black robin alive today is a direct descendant of Old Blue, named for the colour of her identifying leg band. For much of her remarkably long productive life, Old Blue's mate was an equally significant bird, Old Yellow.

The survival of this species was due to an intensive conservation management programme that took advantage of the black robin's breeding system. In September, the black robin male begins to feed his mate as part of courtship. The female builds a nest that is a tidy, open cup of twigs, bark, moss and leaves, felted together by spiderwebs and lined with moss and feathers. The nest is placed in a natural hollow such as a rock crevice or a hollow tree, and even inside abandoned blackbird nests. The female lays between one and three eggs, which she incubates for about eighteen days. Both parents feed the chicks, which fledge after three weeks. A pair of robins often produces two broods a year, and occasionally even three. By removing eggs from Old Blue's nest and fostering them with the related tomtits, the Wildlife Service team led by Don Merton was able to induce her to lay more clutches of eggs.

By 1989, when the population had reached 80 birds, intensive management of black robins stopped, with self-sustaining populations established on Mangere and South East islands.

INSECT EATERS

Noisy flocks of feeding yellowheads, saddlebacks, fantails and parakeets were once a distinctive feature of South Island forests, but are now experienced only on predator-free offshore islands.

YELLOWHEAD
Mohua *Mohoua ochrocephala*

The yellowhead, or mohua, is one of three endemic New Zealand members of the whistler family. Characterised by loud, melodious songs, whistlers occur mainly in Australasia and South-East Asia.

The New Zealand whistlers — yellowheads, whiteheads and brown creepers — are small, arboreal, forest-dwelling insectivores. All three have strong legs, feet that are very large in proportion to their body and powerful toes, and can hang upside down as they carefully search for insects along branches and among leaves. Yellowheads are particularly strong and can hang from one foot as they scratch for insects with the other foot. They also glean in debris accumulated along large branches and in the crotches of tree trunks.

The shafts of the tail feathers project beyond the barbs, and are stiffened to provide a prop. While feeding, yellowheads brace themselves against their tails, gripping the bark with one foot while searching with the other. Yellowheads have a broad, robust pelvis with very strong muscles, allowing them to scratch sideways powerfully, as well as up and down.

During the breeding season the male's call is a loud, musical series of whistles and trills. Outside the breeding season, yellowheads feed in noisy family groups or flocks of up to 25 birds. Showers of falling leaves and debris such as lichen and bark alert observers on the ground to the presence of birds feeding in the canopy.

During the 1800s yellowheads were abundant and conspicuous in beech forests throughout the South Island, as well as in podocarp forests on the West Coast and Stewart Island. Their numbers declined during the 1890s as stoat and rat populations increased, and today they occur in small isolated pockets of beech forest. In beech mast years, the accompanying explosion in mice, rat and later stoat numbers causes a yellowhead population crash, with a disproportionately high loss of females, which are vulnerable as they nest in crevices. Attempts to control predators during mast years are having limited success, and transfers to predator-free islands seem to offer the species better chances. As yellowhead numbers have declined, so have numbers of long-tailed cuckoos, which parasitise yellowhead nests.

INSECT EATERS

A rifleman's call is a very high-pitched zipt-zipt-zipt, which some people find difficult to hear.

RIFLEMAN
Titipounamu *Acanthisitta chloris*

Our smallest bird, the rifleman, is one of two surviving species in the ancient endemic suborder of New Zealand wrens. The New Zealand wrens are believed to have been a very early branch of songbirds that became isolated in New Zealand; the rock wren is the only other surviving species.

Riflemen are small, almost tail-less birds with short, rounded wings and proportionately large legs and feet. Almost entirely insectivorous, they are far more arboreal than the other wrens. Riflemen flick their wings in ceaseless fidgeting as they move up and down tree trunks and along major branches, clinging to vertical trunks and even hanging upside down as they diligently search for food. Their prey includes insects, spiders, flies, moths and caterpillars gleaned from cracks in bark and from mosses and lichens, and they occasionally eat fruit and a little nectar.

Pairs stay in their territory year-round. They begin breeding in September, and the male is very protective of his mate until she has laid. They nest in tiny crevices, too small for rats and stoats to enter, although mice may be a problem. They build a completely enclosed, woven nest with a small side entrance, well lined with feathers. Riflemen usually raise two broods in a season, and both parents share the incubation and chick feeding, assisted by 'helpers' later in the season. The regular helpers are usually unpaired males, which then pair with one of the female offspring they have helped raise. Casual helpers — usually chicks from the first brood — may also help to feed the later brood.

Riflemen were apparently widespread over both main islands at the time of European settlement, but disappeared with the clearance of lowland forest. They remain largely absent from the northern part of the North Island, except for a small remnant population in kauri forest in Northland. They are patchily distributed in native forest and mature scrub in the central and southern North Island, are relatively common in beech and podocarp forests in the South Island, and persist in native-tree town belts in some cities.

Shining cuckoos stay among the foliage and are seldom seen, but have a loud, distinctive call, kui-kui-kui-tiu-tiu-tiu, that they make from high in a tree.

SHINING CUCKOO
Pipiwharauroa *Chrysococcyx lucidus*

New Zealand's parasitic shining cuckoos overwinter in the Solomon Islands, and from late September migrate south to New Zealand, flying directly over the sea. They're swift fliers, and fly even at night.

The cuckoos may feed socially in small groups for the first couple of days after they arrive, and then between six and a dozen birds display communally high in a tree, calling repeatedly and flying from perch to perch. While they're displaying they sit erect, flick their wings out, and wave their wings and tails vigorously.

Shining cuckoos are widespread in the North Island and in the east and north of the South Island. A few make it out to the Chatham Islands, where they parasitise the nests of Chatham Island warblers. They're found in a range of habitats from native forest to willows and wooded gardens, and feed on a variety of insects, especially noxious hairy caterpillars such as those of the magpie moth, which other birds won't eat. They collect several caterpillars in their beaks, squeeze out and swallow the guts, then discard the skins.

Shining cuckoos are dependent on grey warblers (see page 78) to raise their chicks. A female cuckoo lays a single olive-brown egg which develops quickly amid the warbler's clutch of pink-speckled eggs. The cuckoo chick has a hollow in its back that it uses to push the warbler eggs or chicks out of the nest. It positions itself under an egg, then it rests its head against the bottom of the nest, stiffens its neck and reaches behind with its wings to gain extra leverage, and pushes upwards until it levers the egg out of the nest. The cuckoo chick then holds onto the bottom of the nest tightly with its toes so it can't be ejected, and noisily begs for food. The warbler pair may feed the chick up to fifteen times an hour on caterpillars, moths, beetles and leafhoppers.

Between February and April, shining cuckoos gather in large feeding flocks prior to their northward migration. On their return trip some birds fly up the east coast of Australia, and over Lord Howe and Norfolk islands.

INSECT EATERS

When the first International Red Data Book *detailing the world's endangered species was published in 1971, saddlebacks were the only species to receive a 'green page' listing: at that time it was the only threatened species unequivocally saved by direct human intervention.*

SADDLEBACK
Tieke *Philesturnus carunculatus*

Saddlebacks are bright, noisy members of the New Zealand wattlebird family. The North Island species has a faint gold line along the leading edge of the bright chestnut saddle across its back. Juvenile South Island saddlebacks are a uniform chocolate-brown for their first year; some early observers believed these 'jackbirds' were a separate species.

Like other wattlebirds, saddlebacks are poor fliers, and are reluctant to fly across water wider than 250 metres. Powerful muscles attaching the back of the saddleback's broad bill to the skull allow it to open its bill strongly as it forages beneath bark and rotten wood for insects such as weta. On Hen Island, North Island saddlebacks live in taraire and kanuka forest, and are noisy, vigorous feeders, often accompanied by fantails and whiteheads.

Saddlebacks are one of New Zealand's great conservation success stories. In the early 1900s, when people were realising the huia was almost extinct, they also became aware that saddlebacks were missing from many areas of mainland New Zealand. Saddlebacks are vulnerable to rat predation, and by the early 1960s North Island saddlebacks were confined to Hen Island in Northland, while South Island saddlebacks were found only on Big South Cape Island and several small islets near Stewart Island. In 1964, a small Wildlife Service team successfully developed new techniques for catching and transferring North Island saddlebacks. Later the same year news came of an enormous irruption of ship rats on Big South Cape Island, which was the only home not just of the South Island saddleback, but also Stead's bush wren and the Stewart Island snipe. Equipped with recently acquired mist nets the team was able to catch 36 saddlebacks and keep the wild birds alive in aviaries until they could be released on Kaimohu and Big (or Stage) islands off Stewart Island. Sadly, despite great efforts, the bush wren and the snipe became extinct.

Since those early transfers, further relocations of both North and South Island saddlebacks have been made to predator-free islands. There are now more than 6000 North Island saddlebacks, on at least twelve islands, and more than 1200 South Island saddlebacks on a further fifteen islands.

INSECT EATERS

Moreporks roost during the day in dark, quiet places, camouflaged by their drab feathers. If they are discovered by small, day-active birds they can be mobbed, to persuade them to move elsewhere.

MOREPORK
Ruru *Ninox novaeseelandiae*

The morepork is a New Zealand native that belongs to the primitive and ancient hawk-owl, or *Ninox*, genus. Medium-sized owls of this genus are also found in Australia, New Guinea and many Pacific islands. Many of them are restricted to individual islands, and don't occur where other owl species are present. For example, the Lord Howe Island boobook, closely related to the New Zealand morepork, became extinct by 1940, almost certainly as a result of the introduction of masked owls from mainland Australia in the 1920s.

Moreporks live in native forest and well-forested cities such as Wellington, and have a distinctive, familiar call, from which they get their various names. Maori interpreted their call as *ruru*, while Europeans heard it as *morepork*. The birds will respond to people imitating their calls by coming close to investigate.

Moreporks eat invertebrates including large moths (such as puriri moths) and wetas, as well as small rodents and birds. They are opportunistic hunters that catch prey any way they can: as well as hunting on the ground they will catch insects in flight and around street lights, birds on the nest and bats at a roost. Prey is swallowed whole and head first, but only the nutritious parts are digested. Indigestible bones, teeth, claws, beaks and skulls are fashioned in the stomach into sausage-shaped pellets that are encased in fur and regurgitated.

Moreporks and other owls are much more vocal than daytime birds of prey. They communicate at night over long distances with a well-developed vocabulary of calls. Although many species look similar, local names for the hawk-owls reflect distinctive calls that differ in note and cadence. Tropical owl calls are so unique that in the last twenty years field scientists have realised that if owls in different regions have different calls, there is a strong likelihood they are different species. As a result of this call recognition, the number of owl species in the world increased from 123 recognised species in 1980 to 189 by 2000.

Moreporks are monogamous, and nest in holes, trees or perching plants. Incubation is carried out by the female alone, but the male provides food to the female from before egg-laying until the young no longer need to be brooded.

INSECT EATERS

No one knows how long kiwi have been in New Zealand, and whether they walked, flew or rafted here. The fossil record is unhelpful; the oldest kiwi fossil is only one million years old.

BROWN KIWI
Apteryx mantelli

In 1813, the first picture of a brown kiwi published in Europe showed such an unlikely combination of features for a bird that some people thought it was a hoax. For the kiwi is a flightless bird that is, in some ways, more like a mammal: its feathers are shaggy and hair-like, it has cat-like whiskers on its face, nostrils near the tip of a long bill, large, prominent ear openings, no tail, tiny vestigial wings that are scarcely larger than a bent matchstick, powerful legs and an unusual cone-shaped body.

Kiwi behaviour is equally unusual: they are nocturnal predators that hunt with a highly developed sense of smell; eat worms, arthropods and even freshwater crayfish; use smelly droppings as scent marks; lay huge eggs; and have reversed sex roles during incubation.

But far from being a hoax the kiwi is a remarkable one-off design that could only have evolved in the absence of mammals. New Zealand soils were rich in invertebrates, and in the absence of insectivorous mammals kiwi evolved to harvest these riches. They developed a long beak to probe in the soil and detect food by smell, using nostrils at the tip of the beak, and possibly by vibration.

Kiwi belong to a group of flightless birds known as ratites, most of which are much larger and live alongside modern mammals. Kiwi are most closely related to emus and cassowaries, and more distant relatives include ostriches, rheas and the extinct moa of New Zealand. Largely southern hemisphere birds that probably evolved on the prehistoric continent of Gondwana, all ratites share a similar arrangement of palate bones in their mouth.

Taxonomically, kiwi belong to an order of birds found only in New Zealand. There were once five species of kiwi: North Island and South Island brown, the now very rare Okarito brown, little spotted and great spotted kiwis.

Kiwi lack strong flight muscles, and have a very reduced sternum with no keel. As a result their chest is weak and easily crushed, and adults are very easily injured by dogs. Chicks are extremely vulnerable to predation by stoats. Formerly widespread and abundant, brown kiwi now have a scattered distribution and populations continue to decline.

Victorian conservationist Richard Henry described little spotted kiwis as shy, gentle birds, whose survival depended on their ability to hide in quiet places.

LITTLE SPOTTED KIWI
Apteryx owenii

Little spotted kiwi are half the size of brown kiwi, have a shorter, straighter bill and are less raucous and aggressive. They have soft, shaggy, grey plumage mottled with white, and their legs and beaks are off-white to pale pink.

Little spotted kiwi are omnivorous and eat fruit such as hinau berries as well as worms, beetle larvae, cicadas and weta. They were once widespread through the North and South islands, but today only 1000 or so birds survive, on Kapiti Island, with small numbers relocated to other islands.

Female little spotted kiwi weigh on average 1–1.5 kilograms, and lay a 300 gram egg. This egg is proportionally heavier and larger than that of any other species of bird, including other kiwi species. Kiwi evolved from a larger ancestor, perhaps the same body size as a small bush moa, and producing a similar-sized egg. To avoid competition with the moa, kiwi gradually decreased in body size, but there was no intense evolutionary pressure for their eggs to get smaller. Indeed, the large eggs have the benefit of allowing the chicks to be well developed when they hatch.

The egg shell is relatively thin and is easily cracked, so to counter the risk of infection from the soil the albumen appears to contain microbial inhibitors and is gelatinous, to keep the large yolk away from the porous shell.

After laying, the female departs to regain body condition, and the male incubates the egg for about 70 days on his own, in a small nest burrow. He may incubate for up to 21 hours at a time, but might be away for up to ten hours when foraging. He covers the nest entrance with twigs and leaves to conceal it from predators such as weka, but during his long absences the egg cools considerably, which may contribute to the extended incubation period. On hatching, the chick already weighs more than eight percent of an adult's weight. It stays in the burrow with the male for about two weeks, usually foraging independently at night, although it may be brooded during the day. Finally the male abandons the nest, and the chick leaves a day or two later to find its own daytime shelter.

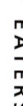

When disturbed into flight, snipe have an explosive, almost quail-like take-off and a characteristic zigzag flight.

NEW ZEALAND SNIPE
Coenocorypha pusilla

New Zealand's eight closely related endemic species of snipe are exceptional in many ways. Although classified with sandpipers in the *Charadriformes* group of waders, they are sedentary birds that prefer forested or thickly vegetated habitats. Compared to the rest of the world's sixteen snipe species, which are more typical migratory waders, ours are considered primitive 'living fossils'.

Formerly widespread throughout the North and South islands, species of New Zealand snipe now survive only on the predator-free island groups of the Snares, Chatham Islands, Antipodes Islands and Auckland Islands, with another species discovered in 1997 on a small rock stack near Campbell Island.

Snipe have very rigid skulls, with their eyes set higher and further back than most other birds. This allows them to have a very broad field of vision. Ear holes located below their eyes allow them to hear when they have their beaks plunged into soil. Their plumage is cryptic, intricately patterned with buff, brown and black. They prefer areas of dense cover and are active day and night, although they may come out of the forest at night to feed in the open. They feed on the ground, probing continuously to find invertebrates and seeds.

Snipe have short legs and a typical crouching stance. Their wings are shorter and broader than other members of the sandpiper group, but although they can fly strongly they usually only do so when displaying or when disturbed. Their tails are short, with stiff, strong outer feathers. Males splay these feathers at right angles during nocturnal territorial flights, producing a distinctive 'chain-rattling' vibration. Muttonbirders on Big South Cape Island attributed this noise to a mythical creature called the hakuwai. Said to be the father of the sooty shearwaters or muttonbirds, the hakuwai would fly over the island in autumn, calling his children away on their northern winter migration. The call of the hakuwai has not been heard over Big South Cape since snipe became extinct there in 1964, although it has been heard on the Chatham Islands. Males also call in response to other males advertising their territories, with a loud, churring *queeyoo-queeyoo*.

Weka have a curious nature. Athough they are shy and often seen only fleetingly as they move between cover, they quickly habituate to people and become bold enough to eat from people's hands and steal bright, shiny objects that take their fancy.

WEKA
Gallirallus australis

Weka are a contradictory rail. They are wily native predators — New Zealand's cheeky avian equivalent of cats — yet they have disappeared from many parts of their natural range, and are now a threatened species. Introduced predators such as cats, rats and mustelids compete with weka for food as well as killing them, and loss of habitat and intensified agricultural practices have contributed to their demise in many places.

Also known as woodhens, Maori hens and kelp hens, all four subspecies of weka have suffered local extinctions and overall declines in population. North Island weka disappeared during the 1920s and 1930s, eventually surviving only around Opotiki. Buff weka became extinct in the eastern South Island during the 1920s but were introduced to the Chatham Islands, where they are now so common they are legally hunted. Stewart Island weka are sparse on Stewart Island itself, although they are locally common on some of its offshore islands. The western weka still occurs on the West Coast in Fiordland and in northwest Nelson, but is rare in between.

That this distinct flightless rail is so at risk is unexpected because many things about its lifestyle mean it should be a good survivor. Weka chicks are nearly full grown between six and ten weeks old, can breed when they are just five months old and, if conditions are suitable, a pair of weka will breed year-round, producing up to four broods a year. The female incubates the eggs during the day, and her mate incubates at night.

When the chicks are three or four months old, weka parents drive them out of their territory. Although they are flightless the young birds will travel long distances — up to 9 kilometres — on foot. They are also good swimmers, and can easily swim up to a kilometre across open sea, rivers or lakes. They have an incredible homing ability; one North Island weka escaped during a relocation attempt and travelled 130 kilometres home.

Weka are opportunistic feeders; about half their diet is plant food, but they will also scavenge fur seal placentas, turn over beached kelp looking for sandhoppers, catch rats and mice, forage in leaf litter and use their sharp bills like jackhammers to break bird eggs, snail shells and the skulls of small birds, including weka chicks.

INSECT EATERS

2

High country

Although active mainly during the day, falcons have been observed hunting soon after dark. Fossil bones show their prey once included short-tailed bats and petrels.

FALCON
Karearea *Falco novaeseelandiae*

New Zealand used to have three endemic day-active predatory birds, but the New Zealand falcon is the only survivor. The extinct *Harpagornis*, the largest known eagle in the world, preyed on large moa, while Eyles's harrier, also an extinct giant of its kind, ate small moa, pigeons, kokako and kaka. Predation by all three raptors influenced the evolution of flightlessness, nocturnal or forest-floor dwelling habits, drab colouration and hole nesting among New Zealand birds.

While harriers are cautious around people, falcons are bold and fearless. Their fierce nest defence, small size and generalist diet and habitat requirements all enabled the falcon to survive the environmental changes that led to the extinction of the eagle and Eyles's harrier.

New Zealand falcons have shorter, more rounded wings and longer, more slender tails than other species in the cosmopolitan genus *Falco*; this allows greater manoeuvrability as they fly in forest, which is an unusual habitat for falcons. Their rapid wing-beats and almost pigeon-like flapping distinguish falcons from harriers (see page 104), which have a lazier, more gliding flight.

Falcons prey on small birds, although they have been seen taking birds as large as takahe. They also hunt skinks and insects such as dragonflies and beetles that they catch in mid-flight, sometimes apparently just for fun. Huhu beetles are an important food for fledging falcons in some areas. Their predation of domestic pigeons and poultry has frequently led to falcons being shot.

Today, falcons are widespread in the rugged, mountainous areas of all three main islands, as well as on the Auckland Islands, although they are uncommon and localised. There are three forms of falcon, all of which overlap in distribution and can interbreed. A large, pale form exists in the east of the South Island; a small, dark, bush form lives in wet forest in the North Island and western South Island; while a form intermediate in size and colour occurs in Fiordland and on the Auckland Islands.

Young falcons, which have a darker, unspotted plumage, have a wider distribution than breeding birds, and are seen even in Wellington and Dunedin suburbs. Their most distinctive call is a loud *kek-kek-kek-kek*, although they also make chittering noises during courtship, and squeal during disputes.

Although popularly regarded as mountain parrots, kea were once abundant in lowland forests and shrublands in the eastern South Island. With the destruction of these habitats, kea now occur in the lowlands only in the forests of South Westland.

KEA
Nestor notabilis

A kea's bill is a highly adaptable tool: a Swiss army knife that can perform delicate tasks such as gently supporting the head of a tiny chick while precisely guiding small amounts of food down its throat, yet powerful enough to crush fibrous roots, tear flesh and dig the ground. The bill also serves as a third foot, a grappling hook that the kea uses along with its feet as it scrambles over rocks and up steep snow slopes.

Using their bills and feet together gives kea a manual dexterity unrivalled in the bird world. Like humans, kea exhibit both right- and left-handedness.

This bill is one of the most obvious defining features of the parrots, with a downward-curving, slightly hooked upper mandible fitting neatly over the upward-curving lower mandible. The upper mandible joins to the skull with a special kind of hinge which gives it greater mobility and leverage than most other bird bills. The dagger-like bill is mainly used for digging the ground in search of roots, rhizomes and grubs, which along with seeds, fruits, buds and flowers make up their largely vegetarian diet.

However, these highland parrots are also known to eat other birds. Fossil evidence of kea beak-marks on moa pelvic-bones suggests that kea used to feed on moa trapped in swamps or killed by giant eagles. In the Seaward Kaikoura Range they prey on the eggs and nestlings of burrowing Hutton's shearwaters (see page 182), using their bills to crush the chicks' skulls and feeding on their oils and fats.

They've been known to attack sheep in winter, landing on their backs and digging with their beaks to expose fat around the sheep's kidneys; their reputation for attacking sheep meant kea were legally killed in great numbers until they were finally protected in 1986.

Kea are not just dextrous; they are one of the world's most intelligent bird species. They play, co-operate, experiment and curiously test everything in their alpine world: the mountains of the South Island between 600 and 2000 metres altitude.

🕊 *Although they can fly strongly, rock wrens usually only fly a few metres between boulders while they are foraging.*

ROCK WREN
Xenicus gilviventris

Rock wrens are found in alpine and subalpine areas of the South Island, between 900 and 2500 metres altitude. Remarkably for a small bird, they stay in their territories year-round, even when the ground is covered in snow for months on end.

Rock wrens are most common close to the treeline, living among scree and old stable rockfalls interspersed with scrub and cushion vegetation. Secure under a sheltering blanket of snow they spend the winter among boulders, scuttling mouse-like through crevices. They will occasionally pop up to briefly bob up and down on a large boulder and look about, before resuming their almost subterranean foraging. They feed on a variety of invertebrates including beetles, spiders, centipedes and caterpillars, as well as fine grass seeds, and *Gaultheria* and *Coprosma* berries.

Rock wrens may formerly have lived in lowland forests on both main islands, if subfossil material from the North Island has been correctly identified. Even today, they reach the coast on the West Coast of the South Island where boulder-strewn rivers provide suitable habitat. In response to predation pressure, they are patchily distributed from northwest Nelson to Fiordland, along the main divide. As they are a high-altitude species, climate change is expected to affect their winter survival and habitat quality, especially with increasing numbers of predators such as rats and stoats.

Like riflemen (see page 44), their only living relative, rock wrens build a large, enclosed, woven nest with a side entrance, in a bank or rock crevice or in dense vegetation such as a flax bush.

Although they are tiny, the endemic New Zealand wrens are ancient members of New Zealand's avifauna, and are as distinctive as moa. Both groups evolved into new species during the late Oligocene period, when New Zealand was reduced to a number of low-lying islands. Four of the six species of New Zealand wren are now extinct: the large, flightless stout-legged wren lived on both main islands until the end of the nineteenth century, and the flightless long-billed wren, the rarest of all fossil bird species, is known from just a few sites. The last Lyall's wren was seen on Stephens Island in 1894, and the last bush wren was seen in 1972 on Kaimohu Island.

Takahe are active at dawn and dusk, as well as through the night. They live in dense cover so they are very vocal, dueting and chorusing to remain in touch.

TAKAHE
Porphyrio hochstetteri

Takahe are a spectacularly eccentric member of the rail family. They're giants that live in an alpine grassland environment, and are long-lived slow breeders. For a hundred years they were considered extinct, until Dr Geoffrey Orbell rediscovered them in Fiordland in 1948.

South Island takahe probably evolved from purple swamp-hens that flew to New Zealand about 25 million years ago, and in a safe island environment they quickly lost the ability to fly. The extinct North Island takahe, known as moho, evolved more recently from a later arrival. It was also flightless, but had longer legs and a weaker bill than its more robust South Island relative.

In many ways takahe are typical rails: they hide in dense snow tussock, are often found near tarns and in wet areas, and can swim well, even hiding underwater for several minutes if they feel threatened. In sunny weather they often sunbathe with their wings outstretched. Their plumage is dark blue across the body and green on their back, and they have a bright, pinkish-red bill and legs. Their strong legs, feet and bills are used as weapons when they fight. They often bob their head as they walk, and flick their tails, especially when they are nervous or alert.

Takahe have large, strong beaks that have evolved to pull out individual tussock shoots. As well as eating the bases of these, they eat mountain daisies, herbs and fern roots.

Takahe are typically monogamous, although they sometimes breed in groups of two females and two or more males. Both sexes share the incubation of the two-egg clutch. Chicks stay with their parents for the first year or two; in a difficult alpine environment it's important that the chicks learn about feeding areas, especially in winter when they may need to migrate to lower altitudes to find food.

Although takahe can breed when they are one year old, young birds that don't breed stay with their parents and share the next season's chick-rearing duties. Chicks are black and downy when they hatch, with black-grey bills and legs, and although they are initially fed invertebrates they soon become primarily herbivorous.

Takahe are threatened, and after their decline to a low of about 100 birds, intensive management has seen their numbers climb to around 200.

3

Town and country

🕊 *On sunny days blackbirds can often be seen sunbathing on the ground with their wings spread, feathers ruffled, bills open and eyes closed.*

BLACKBIRD
Turdus merula

Blackbirds belong to the thrush family, the most widespread and familiar group of perching birds in the world. Many species in this family have very musical calls, and the group includes beautiful songbirds such as nightingales and English robins. The blackbird's call is a rich, mellow, melodious warble, without the song thrush's habit of repetition.

The thrush family has its origins in eastern Asia, where the greatest variety of species is still found. The 300 species in this diverse group occur naturally almost everywhere, including many islands. These birds have naturally colonised even remote island archipelagos such as Hawai'i and Tristan da Cunha, where unique forms have evolved, but didn't reach Australia or New Zealand. They can be found in wooded habitats from temperate to tropical areas, and from urban to mountain habitats.

Blackbirds are widely distributed in Eurasia, from the Palaearctic to the Mediterranean. They can cope with cold, and are found in mountainous areas in the north of Europe and in the Himalayas. In the wild they breed in forests with a bushy undergrowth and soft, grassy ground, and they have become a common bird in cities where they breed in wooded parks and gardens.

Both blackbirds and song thrushes (see page 74) were introduced to New Zealand in the 1860s for sentimental reasons, and were well established by 1900. Blackbirds are now widespread here, in most habitats including dense native forest and inner cities. They feed on invertebrates found in damp grass and among leaf litter, and on fruit such as apples both on the ground and on trees, but they specialise in feeding on earthworms. When feeding on a mown lawn they stay close to cover, hop and then stop to listen for worms with their heads cocked. They gradually close in on a worm, which they are very skilled at removing from its burrow. Blackbirds have done well in New Zealand because of the high concentration of worms here; fourteen species of introduced worms are widespread on pastoral land, and the 178 species of native worms explain why blackbirds thrive in native forest.

The song thrush's territorial song is a long series of clear, deliberately repeated phrases. Its alarm call is sharp and staccato.

SONG THRUSH
Turdus philomelos

All thrushes, including the song thrush that was introduced to New Zealand from its natural range of Eurasia, are able to sing more than one note at a time and have highly developed and complex songs. They are also excellent mimics.

Thrushes occur in mixed broadleaf or conifer forests with shrubby undergrowth and a ground cover of grasses and mosses, in parks and in well-vegetated gardens, where they easily habituate to people and become quite tame. They don't adapt to urban areas or native forest as well as blackbirds. In Europe, song thrush numbers are declining because of uncontrolled hunting in continental Europe, where they are a traditional delicacy, and the widespread use of insecticides.

Thrushes remain as pairs and are strongly territorial year-round. They build substantial cup-shaped nests of dry grass strengthened with mud mixed with decayed wood and saliva. The nests are placed in well-concealed sites in bushes or trees, and also in buildings, crevices, rock walls and on ledges. This wide variety of nest sites is one of the features of the thrush family. In New Zealand, thrush nests are often reused by bush robins on the mainland, and by black robins on the Chathams; the much smaller robins use the old thrush nests as a base, and build their new nests inside (see page 40). A pair of thrushes may raise a number of broods in a year. The female incubates the eggs, and both birds feed and rear the chicks.

Thrushes typically feed on invertebrates including worms and snails, as well as fruit. They are snail specialists, breaking open the shells by hammering them against an anvil such as a rock or a concrete path. They may bring snails some distance to a favourite anvil. As well as eating garden snails, mud snails, flax snails and even marine snails, they pose a threat to some of New Zealand's large, thin-shelled native carnivorous snails.

Although the extinct New Zealand piopio is often called the New Zealand thrush, it was not a member of the thrush family, and is instead regarded as a whistler, the family to which yellowheads belong (see page 42).

🕊 *Despite their success worldwide, starling populations in their native Europe and United Kingdom have been declining, probably due to changing agricultural practices.*

STARLING
Sturnus vulgaris

The 114 species in the starling group include one of the world's most successful birds, as well as one of the most endangered, the Bali starling.

In 1890 several pairs of European starlings were introduced into Central Park in New York, as part of a campaign to introduce all the birds mentioned in Shakespeare's plays to the United States. They are now one of the commonest and widespread birds in the United States, and in places have reached pest proportions. Large flocks have caused at least one plane crash. They were also introduced to South Australia, New Zealand and many tropical islands, and in each place the story is the same: released from the ecological restraints that limited their numbers and distribution in Europe, starling populations have exploded.

Starlings were often introduced to control agricultural pests, as they dwell around farmland in spring and summer, feeding on grass grubs, leatherjackets and other insect larvae. Starlings have a highly specialised feeding technique to reach buried larvae: they insert their closed bills into the soil, then open them forcefully to create holes in which they can probe. They will also perch on the backs of sheep and cattle, waiting for insects to be disturbed; this casual relationship is reminiscent of another species of starling, the oxpecker, which forages for ticks and lice on large African mammals such as giraffes. Starlings also feed on nectar, such as that of flax flowers.

Starlings are very gregarious. They breed in colonies, feed in flocks, and outside the breeding season roost communally in safe locations such as trees or on islands. Overseas, they have been recorded in flocks numbering more than a million birds. These flocks can darken the sky as they return to their night-time roosts in an amazing spectacle of precision flying, with the entire flock wheeling and circling synchronously.

Male starlings are polygamous, and mate with two to five females. Starlings nest in holes in trees, cliffs and road cuttings, buildings and even letterboxes. They are easily attracted to nest boxes which farmers place on fenceposts in an effort to encourage starlings to control grass grubs.

Grey warblers may forage with mixed flocks of other small forest birds.

GREY WARBLER
Riroriro *Gerygone igata*

New Zealand's endemic grey warbler is related to a group of small, fine-billed Australian warblers that used to be known as fairy warblers. The Greek name for this genus of small, drab insectivores is *Gerygone*, which means 'born of sound'.

The grey warbler is well known as a harbinger of spring for its familiar song, which is a sweet, plaintive, silvery 'falling leaf' melody in a minor key. The famous Maori saying 'I hea koe i te tangihanga o te riroriro?' translates as 'Where were you when the riroriro sang?', meaning 'What were you doing in the spring when you should have been planting crops?'

Grey warblers feed singly, in pairs or in small family groups. They are incessantly active, fluttering around foliage, both high and low. This foraging behaviour is unmistakeable and unique in New Zealand, but is similar to other *Gerygone* warblers in Australia. They hover outside foliage with their tails spread, revealing conspicuous white spots at the tip of the tail, and take leaf insects such as caterpillars and flying insects with audible snapping of their bills.

Grey warblers are one of the few native passerines to do well in modified habitats in cities and rural areas, as well as in forest and scrub, from sea level to the bush line. The Chatham Islands have their own warbler, which is heavier and more boldly marked than the grey warbler and needs pristine habitat. Sub-fossil evidence suggests grey warblers were widespread before the arrival of Europeans, but not as abundant as they are today. They have benefited from the loss of other insectivorous birds and on Little Barrier Island, for example, which still has an intact native bird community, they are less common.

Grey warblers are the only New Zealand host for the shining cuckoo (see page 46). The first warbler clutches of the season are laid and reared before shining cuckoos return to New Zealand in late spring, but second clutches are often parasitised by the larger cuckoo. The single cuckoo egg develops very quickly and the larger cuckoo chick pushes the warbler chicks out of the nest, then the warbler parents work frantically to feed a chick that is easily twice their size.

Silvereyes make a rich, warbling song at dawn, and a high-pitched plaintive note keeps flock members in contact.

SILVEREYE
Tauhou *Zosterops lateralis*

Silvereyes are recent self-introduced arrivals in New Zealand. The first record of silvereyes here was at Milford Sound in 1832 — a small flock that had been blown about 2000 kilometres from Tasmania. Their Maori name tauhou means stranger, and they are also commonly called waxeyes or white-eyes.

Until the 1860s there were frequent reports of small flocks of silvereyes, always seen in winter. They probably began breeding here during the 1850s, and started spreading north. The silvereye's natural range is from Western Australia east to Fiji. They are now found throughout New Zealand, where they forage in gardens and along forest edges, eat fruit and aphids in orchards, and flock to bird tables.

The white-eye family of which silvereyes are a member comprises 88 species of small birds that are usually green with distinct white eye rings. They are found in Africa, Asia, New Guinea and Australia and have colonised many islands in the southwest Pacific. Isolated populations on islands or mountain tops have evolved into new forms, often increasing in size and becoming more drab. White-eyes generally have short, pointed bills and brush-tipped tongues for collecting nectar. They are generalists and feed on a wide range of foods: as well as feeding on nectar they search for insects and spiders in foliage and small crevices, and eat berries and fruit.

They often move and forage in small flocks. Their flocking behaviour and ability to exploit a wide range of food resources means they can reach and survive on small forested islands, where many passerines would fail.

Silvereyes mate for life, and pairs often perch together and preen. They defend a small breeding territory, and build a deep, cup-shaped nest. The nest is woven from fine grasses and rootlets, and is suspended hammock-like in a fork between small upper branches.

In New Zealand silvereyes carry avian malaria and bird pox, but appear to be resistant to both. After long periods of isolation, however, island silvereyes often become vulnerable to introduced predators and disease. When rats were introduced to Norfolk Island during the 1920s, populations of the slender-billed silvereye were greatly reduced, and the white-chested silvereye, which is the largest white-eye in the world, is almost extinct.

House sparrows were introduced to New Zealand in 1867 to control insect pests such as grass grubs, but they preferred to eat wheat and within fifteen years had been declared a pest.

HOUSE SPARROW
Passer domesticus

House sparrows have been introduced to New Zealand, Australia, North America and the Pacific Islands, and are rarely found breeding away from human habitation. Widespread through Eurasia and North Africa, eighteen of the 36 species of Old World sparrows are now so associated with humans and cultivated areas that it's impossible to work out their original natural ranges.

In fact, some individual sparrows may never come into contact with any natural space; there are reports of sparrows living and breeding 600 metres underground in a Yorkshire mine, while other birds spend their entire lives inside large buildings such as factories and stores.

Although they are ground-feeding seed-eaters with a preference for cereals, rice and plant buds and insects during the breeding season, in cities they can exist solely on bread and household scraps. Sparrows often feed in large flocks, and may also build their nests together. The grassy nests are bowl- or dome-shaped and have a side entrance. They may be built in holes in trees, rock walls and under roofs, eaves or spouting, and several nests may be built on top of each other.

House sparrows mate for life, and although basically monogamous they have a social courtship display that is often called a 'sparrow wedding'. One male begins displaying to his mate by puffing out his chest to show off his black bib. The size of a male's bib is a badge of his age and experience. With his wings flared and tail cocked he bows to the female and cheeps, and she in turn bobs around and pecks him. Other cock sparrows are attracted by the male's chirping and noisily join in, until eventually the female flies off, pursued by all the males. Although the female's original partner is generally the one to mate with her, between 10 and 20 percent of chicks are fathered by males outside the pair. The female does most of the incubation, although her mate helps a little bit.

Although house sparrows have long been one of the most widespread birds in the world, in Europe and the United Kingdom their numbers have recently declined by more than a quarter.

Hedge sparrows are quiet, sedentary birds, with a slight shuffling gait as they forage on the ground for insects, using their beak to flick aside dead leaves and debris. They add seeds and berries to their diet in winter.

HEDGE SPARROW
Prunella modularis

While the hedge sparrow may superficially resemble the house sparrow in size and colouring, it is much more slender, with a finer bill, and actually belongs to a group of thirteen species called accentors. To avoid confusion, it is often called a dunnock.

The accentors are typically poorly known Palaearctic mountain birds, but the dunnock is a widespread exception found throughout Europe. Dunnocks were introduced to New Zealand several times between 1867 and 1882. They are now locally common, and widespread from Northland to Campbell Island.

This unspectacular reddish-brown bird with a grey belly is secretive, but well studied, and turns out to have a sex life that is anything but drab and dull. It is in fact a spectacular example of the battle of the sexes. In England, where most of the research has been carried out, it's been discovered that dunnocks have a variety of pairing arrangements, including one male with several females, one female with several males, and several males with several females. Monogamy — one male with one female — is often just a compromise that a pair of birds finally settle on. These different relationships reflect a conflict between what's in the best interests of a male (fathering as many chicks as possible) and the best interests of a female (choosing the fittest, strongest males to father her chicks, and getting as much help as possible to raise them).

In spring, during breeding, males make a distinctive shrill *tseep* call. Dunnocks have a fascinating pre-sex display. The female droops her wings, raises her tail and vibrates from side to side. The male stands behind her, bouncing, and pecks at her cloaca for a minute or so at a time, up to 30 times in a row. This eventually stimulates her to eject a drop of fluid containing sperm from any previous matings. The male may repeat this every hour for up to ten days to flush out any sperm from other males, thus increasing his own chances of a successful mating.

When the female finally nests, she builds a neat, hair-lined cup in low vegetation, and lays up to four gem-like pure turquoise-blue eggs.

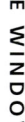

🕊 The goldfinch is the only finch that has a bill fine enough to reach the seeds inside teasel flowerheads. Although a male goldfinch's bill is just one millimetre longer than that of a female, this tiny difference means he is four times more likely to successfully reach the seeds.

GOLDFINCH
Carduelis carduelis

Goldfinches have a fine, tweezer-like bill that they use for picking seed from plants in the *Asteraceae* family, such as thistles and dandelions. They are one of 136 species of Cardueline finch.

The Cardueline finches evolved in the Old World, and are now distributed across North and South America, Eurasia and Africa. Each finch species has specialised to feed on the seeds of particular plants. For example, in contrast to the fine-billed goldfinch, the English hawfinch has a beak strong enough to crack cherry stones.

Goldfinches are striking to look at: they have distinct red markings on their head, and prominent gold-and-white markings on their wings and tail. They're also renowned for their pure musical song; the male's territorial call is a liquid *tsuitt-witt-witt*. It's no surprise that the collective noun for a group of goldfinches is a charm, or that goldfinches were popular caged birds during the Victorian era. By the end of the nineteenth century, intensive trapping in England had caused their numbers to become dangerously low in the wild, and when the Society for the Protection of Birds was formed it made the saving of the goldfinch one of its first tasks.

Goldfinches were originally found throughout Western Eurasia and North Africa, and were introduced to New Zealand in the 1870s to remind early English settlers of home. They are now widespread across mainland New Zealand and the subantarctic islands, and inhabit the same range of habitats they do in the United Kingdom: low-lying deciduous woodlands, pine plantations, orchards, hedgerows and gardens.

In the breeding season, pair formation may take some time. A male goldfinch first attracts a mate, then the pair chooses a nest site and establishes its territory. The male courts the female near the new nest by partially opening his wings and swaying from side to side, showing off his bright yellow wing flashes. The nest is a fine cup made from mosses and fine grass, and lined with animal hair or feathers; it's small and light, enabling it to be built on the fine outer branches of trees. As these branches are prone to swaying in the wind, the nest is deep to ensure the safety of the eggs.

🕊 *Greenfinch chicks have adapted to high levels of disturbance at the nest by being able to fledge early if necessary. Fledging time is anywhere between eleven and seventeen days after hatching. Up to 85 percent of first clutches fail, but greenfinches may renest three to four times a year.*

GREENFINCH
Carduelis chloris

Greenfinches have strong, robust beaks that enable them to eat anything from tiny seeds to large fruit such as sweet briar hips, as well as blackberries and cereal grain such as wheat. They eat sunflower seeds from both the head and off the ground, fruit off trees, and they're the only finch in the United Kingdom large enough to cope with peanuts on bird tables.

Greenfinches are the largest Cardueline finch introduced to New Zealand, and they're closely related to goldfinches (see page 86). Their original range includes the Palaearctic zone of western Europe, including Scandinavia, and the United Kingdom south and west to northwest Africa and Israel. In summer they inhabit evergreen woods, scrubby farms, shrubby gardens, country churchyards and hedgerows. In winter they expand their range to include stubble fields and rough coastal areas. Their range in the United Kingdom has increased as plantations have been established in formerly treeless areas. In New Zealand they live in similar habitats, and are widely but unevenly distributed. They are highly mobile.

The greenfinch's ability to husk large seeds comes from an ingenious conical bill, a heavily built skull and powerful jaw muscles. The upper palate of a greenfinch's beak has a deep groove running along each side between the edge and a central ridge, into which the edges of the lower jaw fit. When the greenfinch has a large seed to husk, it half closes its beak and uses its mobile tongue to lodge the seed on one side. Large seeds are positioned near the base of the gape, while smaller seeds are positioned closer to the tip of the bill. The lower bill is raised until its sharp edge splits the husk, and the bird then uses its tongue to rotate the seed until the husk is removed completely. Then it swallows the kernel and discards the husk. Greenfinches are so dextrous they can hold several seeds in their bills at once, and husk them one by one, a task that takes just seconds. Although greenfinches will eat small seeds, it is more efficient to eat larger ones.

Greenfinch nestlings are mainly fed regurgitated seeds, along with aphids and caterpillars for the first few days.

In spring, a male chaffinch attracts a mate and establishes a territory with a long musical succession of chip calls, followed by a musical flourish which lasts several seconds. He may repeat this song up to 3300 times a day.

CHAFFINCH
Fringilla coelebs

Despite its name, the chaffinch is not a true finch. It's a 'prototype' seed-eater that sits evolutionarily between the insect-eating songbirds and the true Cardueline finches.

There are only three species in this group: the chaffinch and the brambling are distributed across Eurasia, while the blue chaffinch occurs in the Canary Islands. All are birds of deciduous woodland and forest, with distinctive white shoulder patches and white wing and tail flashes.

The chaffinch is one of Eurasia's commonest birds, found from Mediterranean Africa to western Siberia. It was introduced into New Zealand several times from 1862 onwards and has become one of our most abundant birds, found throughout the mainland and on many offshore islands. The chaffinch seems almost pre-adapted to succeed here; it easily went from eating the seeds of northern beech trees to those of the southern *Nothofagus* beeches, both of which have irregular but abundant mast years. Although they eat only fallen seeds, chaffinches also eat a wide range of insects here, and can be seen hawking over streams for emerging insects such as mayflies.

Built in the forks of branches, chaffinch nests are heavily felted, and so well camouflaged with the lichens found on neighbouring branches that they are almost indistinguishable. They are lined with soft hair and feathers. While the chicks are small the male feeds the female, who in turn feeds the chicks. Both birds feed their older chicks mainly on caterpillars, until they become independent at around five weeks old. Because caterpillars become abundant only in early summer chaffinches have time to raise only one brood a year.

During the European winter chaffinches split into migratory separate-sex flocks and fly away from cold, snowy areas. Females migrate the furthest, leaving the males behind in large bachelor flocks. These bachelors give the chaffinches their species name of *coelebs*, in honour of their celibate status. Although they don't appear to migrate here, it's not uncommon to see bachelor flocks of chaffinches in coastal southern New Zealand in autumn and winter.

Skylark chicks are very cryptic in colour, covered in long, filamentous, khaki-coloured down that resembles wisps of grass.

SKYLARK
Alauda arvensis

Most larks are desert species, but the skylark is a temperate exception. Skylarks have elaborate songs, and it's on account of their beautiful song that more than a thousand skylarks were introduced to New Zealand between 1864 and 1875.

Male skylarks defend their breeding territory against rival males and advertise for mates by singing in flight. The male climbs higher and higher on fluttering wings, until he reaches 50 to 100 metres above the ground and is almost invisible. His song is an incessant outpouring of rapid rolling, chirruping and whistling, with some notes varied and others repeated, for three to fifteen minutes. Then, still singing, the male begins to descend, and at the very end folds his wings and falls swiftly and silently towards the ground. Males remain faithful to their breeding site year after year, and visit and sing for most of the year. They sometimes perch and sing from fence posts.

Skylarks are common in all open country, including sand dunes, farmland and tussock country, and won't forage or nest near tall woodlands or hedges. They have cryptic, streaked brown plumage to conceal them as they feed on the ground. Characteristically there is a white flash on the outer edges of the tail and a thin white trailing edge on the wings that are visible in flight. If disturbed, they might take off and fly low across the ground, but they are just as likely to run, walk or even crouch, relying on camouflage to hide. Skylarks, like pipits and buntings, have a distinctive long claw on the back toe that gives them added stability when they stand on the ground.

Skylarks make masterly use of the contours of the ground to conceal themselves during nesting, tucking their deep, grass-lined, cup-shaped nest in a small hollow such as a hoof print. The four to five eggs are khaki and covered in dense, almost blurred, olive markings. Because of the high risk from predators on the ground, eggs are incubated for only ten to twelve days, and the chicks leave the nest ten days after hatching, even though they won't fly until they are twenty days old.

🕊 *Yellowhammers are wary but not shy. If disturbed, a bird will immediately fly swoopingly to a high vantage point such as a tree, so the usual view is of the departing bird's chestnut-brown rump.*

YELLOWHAMMER
Emberiza citrinella

The yellowhammer is one of our most familiar introduced birds, with a lilting song that is written as *si-si-si-si-si-si-suu*, but better recognised as *a-little-bit-of-bread-and-no-cheese*. During courting the males sing from fenceposts, powerlines or high trees.

There are two kinds of bunting in New Zealand: the yellowhammer, and the closely related cirl bunting (see page 96). More than three quarters of the world's 290 species of bunting evolved in the Americas, but they have spread into Europe and Asia, reaching north into the Palaearctic.

The yellowhammer is a typical bunting with a wide range that includes Scandinavia. It favours more open country than the cirl bunting, preferring open pastures and wooded meadows, and is widespread throughout New Zealand.

The yellowhammer has distinctive golden-yellow feathers and white tail flashes. It has a slightly longer tail than the very similar cirl bunting, and a finer beak, which reflects its diet of small grass seeds. Male yellowhammers have finely patterned, scratchy black markings on their brightly coloured heads.

During the breeding season a male yellowhammer defends a long, thin nesting territory, often along a hedgerow or a cluster of trees. The female makes a woven, cup-shaped nest on the ground in the shelter of the trees, and incubates the eggs on her own, although her mate helps feed insects to their chicks. In winter, the birds' territoriality breaks down, and they can be seen feeding in flocks that can number in the hundreds.

Yellowhammers are not thriving in England; indeed, many of the buntings in North America and Europe have suffered from the increasing industrialisation of farming and the use of pesticides. Many of North America's buntings, which are known there as sparrows, have specialised habitat requirements and have been particularly vulnerable to farming changes. The dusky seaside sparrow was a swamp-dwelling bunting that gained some fame in the 1980s when Disney World in Orlando became involved in a sadly doomed attempt to save it from extinction. The only buntings that continue to thrive are those that live in the remote Palaearctic, away from people.

OPEN COUNTRY

After the cirl bunting's autumn moult, each feather has a soft, buff-coloured tip that helps conceal the bird in the winter landscape.

CIRL BUNTING
Emberiza cirlus

Cirl buntings are one of our most enigmatic introduced birds. They are recluses that spend much of their time out of sight under trees or in long grass, making quiet, repetitive *tzee* calls that are more reminiscent of a cricket than a bird.

They were introduced here from the southwest of the United Kingdom, and are very common in Mediterranean countries with hot, dry climates. In New Zealand they're found in areas with a Mediterranean-type climate, on the drier East Coast and in limestone country, where the highly modified farmland suits their very particular requirements.

Cirl buntings need a mosaic of habitats that includes rough pasture with a plentiful supply of broadleaf weed seeds and lots of insects to feed their young, bushes and hedges to nest in, and plantations of trees, especially deciduous ones.

They are one of two species of bunting now found in New Zealand. A quick glimpse of either a cirl bunting or the related yellowhammer (see page 94) would suggest they were finches, but on closer inspection the drab, finch-sized cirl bunting can be seen to be very un-finchlike. They have a long, slightly forked tail, and a lilting flight that takes them over the tops of long grass and even under cover. As they fly away they reveal a dull, olive-green rump.

Male cirl buntings have distinctive and beautiful black markings on their butter-yellow heads and on their bibs. They are most drab in winter, after moulting in autumn. The buff tips of the post-moult feathers slowly wear away over winter to reveal, by spring, bright, colourful breeding plumage. This plumage made them attractive to caged-bird collectors, who would trap them and display them at shows.

Cirl buntings breed four to six weeks later than the finches, to coincide with the flush of insects that they will feed to their offspring. For the rest of the year they feed mostly on broadleaf weed seeds, using their distinctive fine beaks which have a large lower and a small upper mandible. A lump inside the upper mandible is used to crush seeds.

🕊 *One of our most common birds, redpolls have been seen in the King Country in flocks of up to 100,000 birds.*

REDPOLL
Carduelis flammea

Redpolls are sociable birds, often gathering in noisy flocks to feed on good seed sources. In spring, male redpolls have a distinctive, bouncy display flight, at some height above the ground, which serves to advertise a general breeding colony.

Once pairs are nesting the general breeding display stops, and although males defend nesting territories, a number of birds may forage together in a larger feeding area.

For a small, tidy bird, the redpoll builds a surprisingly untidy, bulky nest. The shallow nest is made of grasses, moss, old flowerheads and rootlets, lined with wool, thistledown or feathers, and located in a secure fork in a tall bush.

Redpolls are birds of open forest, birch woodland and tundra, found in northern North America and Eurasia. In winter, they migrate to lower altitudes and warmer climates, heading to the southern states in North America, and to the Mediterranean and southern Asia. They have the smallest bills of the species of Cardueline finches introduced into New Zealand, adapted for eating small birch and grass seeds. Their European distribution varies slightly each year depending on the availability of birch seeds, and even in New Zealand they remain slightly migratory.

About 500 redpolls were introduced to New Zealand in the 1860s, and by the 1900s they were widespread. They're now found almost everywhere, including most islands and the subantarctic. They are more common in farmland, less-developed areas and tussock grassland up to 1750 metres altitude. Tussock seeds have proved a perfect substitute for birch seeds, so they are particularly common in high, dry areas of the South Island. In some South Island fruit-growing areas they are a pest, damaging spring blossom. Their diet includes the flowers and spring growth of willows, larches and birches, and later in the year the seeds of tussock, sorrel, dandelion and birch.

Redpolls and goldfinches (see page 86) are adept at eating while holding food in one foot and perching on a branch, unlike greenfinches (see page 88), which can only manage food with their feet when they're on the ground. A redpoll can even feed on a dangling birch catkin, by pulling the catkin up against the branch on which it is perching and using its fine bill to pick at the seeds.

Several species of lapwing, including the spur-winged plover, have wattles on their face and distinctive spurs on their wings.

SPUR-WINGED PLOVER
Vanellus miles

Known as spur-winged plovers in New Zealand, and more correctly as masked lapwings in Australia, spur-winged plovers are a very successful recent migrant to New Zealand. They are one of twenty-four species known as lapwings that separated from true plovers tens of millions of years ago, and whose lineage evolved in the southern continents of Africa and Australia.

Lapwings evolved in Africa to become tropical and subtropical inland birds of open spaces, especially grasslands. Nearly half of the world's lapwing species are confined to Africa, and a further two are found in Australasia. Lapwings have broad wings, and fly with conspicuous, exaggerated flaps, which gives rise to their name. Their wings, head and tail are boldly marked in black and white. They feed with the typical plover pattern of run-stop-peck.

Spur-winged plovers have very interesting courtship behaviours. The male makes an aerial display to advertise his territory, tumbling in a butterfly-like flight. He also has a distinctive ground display, in which he hunches and runs at another bird, drooping his wings, fanning his tail and bobbing. This is accompanied by a loud, strident, grating call.

Spur-winged plovers defend their territory strongly, and become very aggressive around their nest, which is a simple scrape lined with grass. They call loudly, and chase and stoop against predators such as harriers, magpies and humans. They also feign injury to draw predators away from their nest or chicks.

Spur-winged plovers bred for the first time in New Zealand at Invercargill Airport in 1932. They spread rapidly: by the 1950s they were found throughout Southland, and by the 1980s they were all through the South Island. They reached the North Island during the 1970s, the Chathams during the 1980s, and by the 1990s they had even made it to the Kermadecs. Individuals have been seen in the Auckland Islands and Antipodes Islands, although they have not established there. There are now estimated to be more than 100,000 of these birds in New Zealand.

Australian magpies are fiercely territorial during the breeding season, and will attack humans that come too close to their nesting territory.

AUSTRALIAN MAGPIE
Gymnorhina tibicen

The Australian magpie is one of fourteen species of cracticids, robust black-and-white or grey songbirds that are native to Australia and New Guinea. They're called magpies because their striking black-and-white plumage is reminiscent of Old World magpies belonging to the crow family.

They are actually closely related to wood swallows, strong hawking birds found in Australia and Asia, but probably evolved from a more predatory ancestor. Australian magpies are the best known members of the cracticid group. Most magpies in New Zealand are white-backed, but around Napier and Hastings the magpies are a less common black-backed form.

Magpies typically inhabit woodland, scrub and grassland in Australia. In New Zealand they are common on farmland and in semi-rural areas, around human habitation. Most people are familiar with their beautiful carolling song, and the birds play an important role in Australian culture. They have also become a feature of the New Zealand natural and cultural landscape, featuring most famously in Denis Glover's poem 'The Magpie'.

Magpies feed on invertebrates and reptiles, which they find by walking and searching on the ground, listening for movement as well as using their keen eyesight. A number of birds may feed communally, all facing and walking in the same direction, but remaining apart and not interacting or interfering with one another. In New Zealand, magpies have expanded their feeding niche to become significant predators of small birds and nestlings. They have been seen persecuting and killing native birds as large as the tui. This is a role they don't have in Australia, where they face too much competition from a number of predatory hawks.

They have strongly curved claws and well-padded toes, reminiscent of those that raptor-like birds use to absorb the impact when they strike their prey. They also have a small but clearly defined hook at the end of their beak which they use to hold and tear prey.

Australasian harriers established in New Zealand only recently, when the clearance of forest created suitable open habitat and the extinction of the giant endemic Eyles's harrier removed competition.

AUSTRALASIAN HARRIER
Kahu *Circus approximans*

Harriers are slim, medium-sized birds of prey, with hooked beaks and talons, long tails and broad wings. They worry prey with a slow, harrying flight low over grasslands, swamps and shrubland. They also hover with slow, powerful wing beats, their long, thin legs dangling ready to grasp prey. In New Zealand they often soar high looking for carrion, which they don't do in their native Australia.

Australasian harriers originally came from tropical and temperate Australia, favouring wetlands in well-watered coastal areas. In New Zealand these hawks have expanded their range to include farmland, high-country slopes and river valleys with tussock and scrub.

Harriers are usually silent, but during their breeding display they utter a high-pitched descending whistle that carries far. Early in the breeding season the male harrier displays over a breeding territory, making shallow, undulating dives that become increasingly steep. He flies up to between 50 and 200 metres above the ground, then dives straight down, pulling out after 20 metres or so into a tight barrel turn. The male may 'stoop' at the female on the wing, causing her to flip over and thrust her claws at him, an action they also make when he is passing food to her. They may occasionally lock talons and spiral downwards before breaking apart, then the male continues with more display dives.

Harriers nest on the ground amid tall vegetation, and may build a floating nest among dense reeds in water up to 1.5 metres deep, to avoid predators such as ferrets and stoats. Until the chicks are half grown the male hunts for food, the female staying with the chicks at the nest, tearing food into small pieces that the young birds pick from her bill. Young hawks are blackish-brown, with males being paler and more grey than females, although both sexes also become more grey with age. They have a distinctive white rump, and as they age their primary wing and tail feathers acquire a blue-grey sheen.

Outside the breeding season harriers may roost communally in groups of up to 30, in long grass, swamps or reed beds. Each bird tramples a platform to stand on, and after spreading out to hunt during the day the birds return to roost together each night.

OPEN COUNTRY

The little owl is classified in the genus Athene, *named after the Greek goddess of wisdom. Its call is a high* kieuw.

LITTLE OWL
Athene noctua

Little owls have a huge range across Eurasia and North Africa, and in 1906 birds from Germany were brought to New Zealand, which is why they are sometimes called German owls.

Less than 3 percent of the world's birds are nocturnal and, of these, more than half are owls. The relationship of owls to other groups of birds is little understood and much debated. The 189 species of owls are all easily recognisable by their distinctive upright stance, rounded shape and large head, with huge, front-facing yellow eyes in saucer-shaped discs of radiating feathers. Their downward-curving beak is short and hooked, and may be difficult to see among the thick feathers. They have powerful, feathered legs and sharp, curved talons. Unlike hawks and falcons, owls prefer to carry their prey in their beaks rather than their talons.

Little owls were introduced to control sparrows and finches, but instead they eat mainly beetles and invertebrates. Their diet also includes worms, snails, frogs, skinks and mice, most of which they hunt and catch on the ground. Little owls are greyish-brown in colour, heavily spotted and streaked with white; overall they are paler and smaller than moreporks (see page 50).

Little owls are a familiar sight in the South Island, in open farmland east of the Southern Alps. They can be active by day, and are often seen perched on fenceposts and telegraph poles, and around tall trees such as macrocarpas. They frequently hunt on the ground, bouncing around as they search for and chase invertebrates, such as chafer beetles emerging after dark. They also hawk for moths and flying beetles around rural street lights. Country roads are favoured places for owls to eat dead insects on the road, and this habit unfortunately results in the carcasses of little owls being a common sight on rural roads in summer.

They breed in hollow trees, between bales stacked in hay barns, in holes in rock walls, disused rabbit burrows, banks and deserted buildings. The female alone incubates the three round, white eggs, but both parents rear the chicks. When the chicks leave the nest 40 days after hatching they are still partially downy, and remain dependent on their parents for another month.

OPEN COUNTRY

🕊 *As well as occurring near waterways, in mangroves and along the coast, sacred kingfishers are often found well away from water in gardens, farmland and even inland forest.*

SACRED KINGFISHER
Kotare *Todiramphus sancta*

Kingfishers are a worldwide group, whose eighty-six species include some specialised fishers, as well as other more primitive forest kingfishers that prey on dry-land species. Forest kingfishers, including New Zealand's sacred kingfisher, almost certainly evolved in the tropical rainforests of northern Australia, and are now found in Australia, Indonesia, New Guinea and many islands across the Pacific.

Kingfishers have large heads with robust, long bills, short necks, stout bodies, and short legs with fleshy feet. The most famous and unusual kingfisher is Australia's kookaburra.

Compared to many other native birds, our sacred kingfisher is a relatively recent arrival. It is regarded as a subspecies, and is slightly larger and more intensely coloured than the Australian form. It is commoner in the warm north of the country than in the south, and has never colonised the Chatham or subantarctic islands.

Sacred kingfishers are usually sit-and-wait predators of small animals, although they sometimes hawk on the wing for dragonflies. Their wide diet includes insects, spiders, worms, molluscs, crustaceans, centipedes, fish, frogs and tadpoles, lizards and even small birds such as silvereyes and small mammals such as mice. Because of their predatory habits they are often mobbed by small birds, including silvereyes and fantails. Kingfishers hunt in woodland and from bushes along rivers, lake edges and seashores. They have keen eyesight and can spot prey up to 90 metres away. To compensate for a limited degree of eye movement, they jerk their whole head back and forth to work out distances.

Kingfishers are monogamous. The male defends a territory such as a patch of forest or a stretch of coast by calling loudly and repeatedly from a conspicuous perch. Kingfishers nest in holes in clay cliffs or riverbanks, and both sexes help dig the nest tunnel. They begin by flying directly into the bank until a hole is partially formed, then they perch and peck to enlarge the tunnel.

The female begins incubating as soon as the first egg is laid, so the eggs hatch at the same intervals at which they were laid — usually a day apart. As a result, the nestlings vary considerably in size, although both parents feed all the chicks equally.

Pheasants are usually solitary birds, although they may band into groups during hard winters. They seldom wander far from their home range.

PHEASANT
Phasianus colchicus

There are forty-eight species of pheasant, and all but one come from Asia, where they live in forest, such as bamboo thickets in China and rhododendron forests in the Himalayas. Although their loud calls are often heard, they are shy birds and are rarely seen.

The pheasant introduced to New Zealand is the ring-necked or common pheasant, comprising a number of widespread subspecies. New Zealand pheasants are descended from three of these subspecies: the Chinese ring-necked pheasant, which has a strong white band around its throat; the Mongolian pheasant, with an incomplete white neck band; and the black-necked pheasant, which lacks a white band. The resulting New Zealand hybrids vary in colour and include a striking dark or melanistic variation of the black-necked pheasant, which is dark metallic green with blue reflections on its neck and flank. Only the male is brightly coloured and patterned, with a long, pointed tail; the smaller females are drab with shorter tails, while juvenile birds are intricately but cryptically marked for camouflage.

Pheasants were introduced on numerous occasions from 1842 onwards, and there are now about a quarter of a million birds, locally common in the north and western districts of the North Island, with small numbers in Nelson, Canterbury and Otago. Because of their popularity as a game bird, thousands of pheasants are bred in captivity and released each year for the express purpose of hunting. Only the males are hunted, and their feathers are also popular for fishing flies.

Like most pheasants, male New Zealand pheasants mate with a number of females, which then incubate eggs and raise chicks on their own. The female nests in dense cover such as blackberry, long grass or dense scrub, and lays between seven and fifteen olive-brown eggs in a hollow lined with sparse vegetation. The flightless chicks eat insects for the first two weeks of their lives, then they learn to fly and gradually adapt to the adult diet of leaves, seeds, grain and large insects.

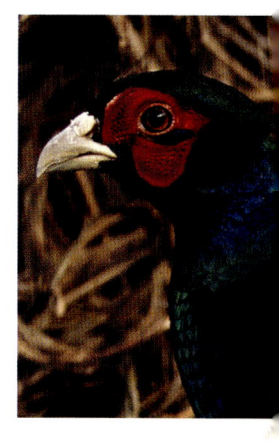

In India, before the summer monsoon arrives in spring, peacocks become solitary and pugnacious, and call loudly and frequently. This timing gave rise to the Hindu belief that peacocks can predict when it will rain.

PEAFOWL
Pavo cristatus

The peafowl is a large, gregarious forest pheasant, yet despite its flamboyant appearance it is a naturally shy bird that hides in undergrowth. It is India's national bird. Revered by both Hindus and Muslims, it is widespread through India and Sri Lanka, and semi-wild birds are a common sight in villages.

The peafowl was introduced to New Zealand in the 1840s for its beauty, and feral birds now inhabit warm, dry, rough country throughout the North Island and in the northwest of the South Island.

The wheel-like tail of the male (or peacock) is a display of 200 iridescent feathers, many adorned by glowing 'eyes'. The number of eyes is related to age: the older the peacock, the more eyes he has on his tail. The most successful peacock of the group, which mates with the greatest number of females, also tends to have the most eyes in his train — a strong signal of his longevity and strength.

Surprisingly, the feathers in a peacock's train — which may be up to a metre long — are not tail feathers. They are the tail coverts, feathers which lie over the tail and are usually small. Under the train the male still has plain brown tail feathers.

Males defend display territories in forest clearings, each less than half a hectare in size and containing between one and four partially enclosed stages or alcoves. A peacock waits until a peahen drifts into sight then fans his tail, making a noisy rattle as he arranges the eyes, but modestly turning away so she sees only the drab underside. He moves his wings rhythmically and slowly encourages her towards an alcove, sure to always keep the drab side of the tail towards her.

Once the peahen is in the alcove the male turns and presses his tail fan forwards over her head, engulfing her in the display of eyes. He shivers, and the fan rustles with a loud, silvery sound. The female becomes completely still and the male turns away and begins moving his wings again. A female may repeat this display many times with this and other males before she chooses one to mate with.

Male turkeys have traditional strutting grounds where they display with fanned tails and swollen wattles, gobbling loudly. Their gobbles can be heard more than a kilometre away.

TURKEY
Meleagris gallopavo

The turkey has always been regarded as American as apple pie, and Benjamin Franklin even proposed them to be America's national bird. However, recent DNA work shows they evolved relatively recently from European pheasants.

Wild turkeys are North America's largest game bird. They are widespread there in forest clearings and in brushland, although at the end of the nineteenth century hunting and forest clearance had brought them to the brink of extinction. Due to successful conservation and reintroduction programmes they are now more numerous than ever. They are a typical pheasant: they're good eating, have strong legs, and are unwilling fliers unless threatened by danger.

Wild turkeys were introduced to New Zealand in 1890 and are common on farms as domestic birds. There are also truly feral flocks on rough farmland in the North Island and in a few South Island areas. The males are larger and have brighter plumage than the females, and mate with a number of females that they attract with elaborate displays.

The female incubates between eight and fifteen cream-and-brown speckled eggs in a leaf-lined scrape in the ground. The chicks leave the nest after one night, and are brooded on the ground by the female for two weeks until they are able to fly and reach roosts in a tree. The brood stays with the mother as a flock for six months, until the males separate into sibling groups. The males fight each other within these groups to establish rank, and sibling groups also fight other sibling groups to establish flock dominance. Later in life the males, which have fighting spurs on their legs, will have to jostle for dominance at a strutting ground.

For the first two weeks of their life, chicks are fed on insects. As adults, turkeys forage on the ground. In the United States they feed mainly on acorns, as well as seeds, nuts, fruits, nuts and tubers, a few invertebrates and even the occasional lizard. In the absence of many acorns in New Zealand they prefer clover, weed seeds and large insects.

🕊 *Helmeted guineafowl cackle raucously and are great guard birds. Farmers frequently put them with chicken flocks to warn of danger.*

HELMETED GUINEAFOWL
Numida meleagris

Guineafowl are related to pheasants, and the six species are all endemic to Africa. All guineafowl have necks and faces bare of feathers but with colourful skin and adorned with wattles. The helmeted guineafowl has a prominent casque on its head, which may serve to shield its brain from the sun.

Helmeted, or tufted, guineafowl were introduced to the Bay of Islands by missionaries, and later to other North Island sites. Today, small feral flocks exist in the Northland, Waikato, Rotorua and Wanganui districts.

Helmeted guineafowl have an unusual monogamous breeding system that is unique among pheasants. As the breeding season approaches there is increased aggression between males in the winter flocks, which eventually causes the flock to break up. Aggressive displays begin with one male approaching another with his head down, hunched over with his wings pressed tight to his sides yet lifted slightly, to appear as large as possible. The second male responds in the same way, then begins to chase the first male. The chase is ritualised and the first male is never caught — the same distance is always maintained between them. The chase is contagious: soon other males join in, following in single file behind the first two birds.

The females, meanwhile, watch the chase, assessing the stamina of the males. Females may 'date' a number of males before settling in a monogamous pairing that will last just one breeding season. This pairing remains strong until the female begins incubating the four to twelve eggs, at which time the male wanders off to associate and possibly mate with unpaired females, although he doesn't court them. However, when the eggs hatch he returns to help the female feed the chicks, a job she couldn't do on her own. For two weeks, until the chicks can fly, he helps to find insects for them. During this period the female broods her young on the ground. As soon as they can fly the young birds begin to roost in trees, eventually expanding their diet to include seeds, bulbs, roots, tubers and fallen grain.

OPEN COUNTRY

California quail have the New World quail's distinctive small, forward-pointing topknot, and a loud emphatic call that sounds like Chi-ca-go.

CALIFORNIA QUAIL
Callipepla californica

California quail come from the western seaboard of North America, where they range from Baja California in the south to British Columbia in the north. They were introduced to New Zealand during the 1860s and 1870s, and are widespread in both the North and South islands. Radiata pines and macrocarpas are other imports from the same slightly humid American coast that have also thrived in New Zealand.

California quail are common in open woodlands, scrubby foothills and stream valleys, and need to be near permanent water. Unlike most other New World quails, they roost only in dense trees or shrubs, not on the ground. In their native California they feed on vetches and other members of the pea family; in New Zealand their diet may include readily available broom and gorse seeds.

California quail nest in low vegetation such as long grass, brush or near hedgerows. The nest is a carefully concealed scrape lined with dead leaves. The female lays up to 22 cream-coloured eggs, patterned with dark chocolate blotches. Although the eggs are conspicuous, the well-camouflaged female sits tight on them throughout incubation. An incubating female can be approached to within a metre, and she won't fly off the nest.

The basic quail social unit is called a covey. A covey is usually a family joined by one or two other individuals, but during autumn and winter in open habitats many coveys may join together in roosting flocks of up to 200 birds.

California and bobwhite quail (see page 120) are very typical examples of New World quails. Like the related domestic chicken, they're rotund, short-legged birds with rounded wings. They are strong runners and rarely fly except to escape danger, when they burst from the ground in an explosion of rapid wing beats. Their short flights are powered by glycogen-burning muscles on their chests which make for good eating, explaining their desirability as a game bird. New World quails are smaller than Old World quails, and are boldly marked in black and white against cryptic background colouration of buff and grey.

The bobwhite quail's flight has been charmingly described as impetuous; it takes off suddenly into whirring flight on short, stubby wings.

BOBWHITE QUAIL
Colinus virginianus

The bobwhite quail might be little known in New Zealand, but in Virginia in the United States it has long been considered the king of game birds. That's quite a claim for a bird that weighs only 180 grams, but game hunters consider it to be an exciting target.

Bobwhite quail, also known as Virginia quail, are found in brushland and open woodland in the eastern United States. More than 400 bobwhite quail were released throughout New Zealand in 1898, followed a year later by a further 750. But unlike the California quail (see page 118), after a few successful years most bobwhite quail disappeared during the early 1900s. By the 1950s just a few remained in the wild on the East Coast of the North Island at places such as Gisborne and Wairoa, although some were maintained in captivity in game parks. It may be that the new immigrants were not released in the most suitable places, and perhaps they would have thrived in pine forests if they had been more common then.

A handful of people are now breeding and releasing bobwhite quail onto pasture around Timaru and Ashburton. The birds are reared in moveable coops. When the time comes the coops are moved to the release site and the doors are opened, allowing the birds to leave in their own time. They can continue to return to the coop, entering and leaving through a port in the roof to safely feed out of reach of predators.

Bobwhite quail get their name from their rising, whistled *bob-white* call. At night groups of up to 20 birds roost together in tight bunches on the ground, with their heads facing outwards. If disturbed, they explode into flight.

The bobwhite quail has also been declining in its previous stronghold, the eastern United States, where numbers dropped by nearly two thirds between 1966 and 1993. The species is one of early succession agricultural habitats, and depends on a patchwork farming landscape that includes fallow fields, cutover woodlots and weedy patches. Its decline in the United States has been caused by changing farming practices, especially the move to large, industrialised farms.

OPEN COUNTRY

Brown quail are almost tail-less, and their plumage is beautifully cryptic. Their brown feathers are streaked with fine white markings.

BROWN QUAIL
Synoicus ypsilophorus

The brown quail is a typical Old World quail. Old World quails are very different from New World quails like the California and bobwhite quails; many are nomadic, even migratory, and they may be partly nocturnal.

Occurring in the grasslands of Asia, Africa and Australasia, Old World quails comprise six 'super-species', each of which contains many, very widely distributed subspecies. Brown quail are widespread in eastern Indonesia, Papua New Guinea and Australia, where they are sometimes called swamp quail. Found around the damper edges of Australia, the species doesn't occur in the arid interior, although occasionally after very heavy rains the birds will migrate temporarily inland. In New Zealand they prefer areas of low, swampy ground, rank vegetation, heavy pasture and coastal scrub.

Brown quail were released into New Zealand from Australia many times during the 1860s and 1870s. Although releases in the South Island never succeeded, brown quail are moderately common in the top half of the North Island, and are abundant in Northland. They are often seen at dawn and dusk, in coveys of six to ten birds, dust-bathing on gravel roads. Brown quail are very small, plump birds, and eat the seeds of native plants, cereals, legumes and weeds.

Their close relative, the stubble quail, is widespread in Australia's drier areas. Stubble quail are streaked with heavy white markings, and have a cinnamon throat patch. They are very closely related to the now-extinct New Zealand quail, which resembled them strongly. A quarter of the world's more than 200 quails and pheasants are now rare or endangered, but the endemic New Zealand quail has the sad distinction of being the only species which has become extinct, as a result of habitat destruction and predators, particularly ship rats.

4

Wetlands and rivers

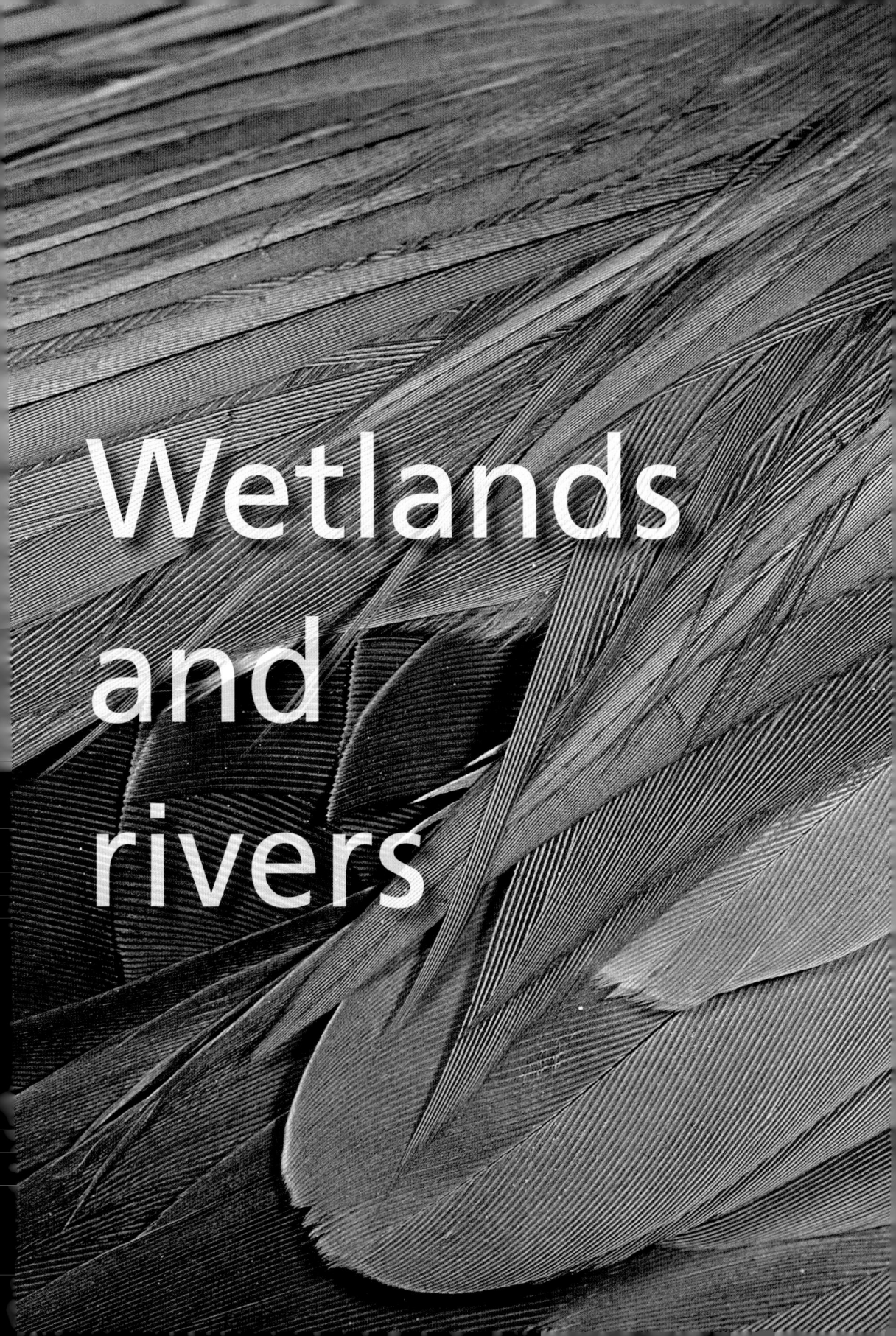

Wrybills, like plovers, have sharp eyesight and have a typical foraging style: a repetitive run-stop-peck.

WRYBILL
Ngutu parore *Charadrius frontalis*

The endemic New Zealand wrybill is famous for being the only bird in the world that has a bill that bends sideways to the right. The end of the bill is already bent when the chick hatches, and it's perfectly adapted for snipping up stream insects that hide under stones, away from the light. Wrybills also use their bills to scythe sideways through silt and mud in search of crustaceans.

Their unusual bills aside, wrybills are typical plovers. There are 41 species of true plover, which in New Zealand we call dotterels; the plover group also includes 24 species of lapwing. Typically smaller than lapwings, such as spur-winged plovers (see page 100), true plovers have moderately long legs, short bills, round heads and large eyes.

The plover group has a large southern hemisphere bias. Six genera occur in Australia, three in South America and one in Africa, while there are only three genera in the northern hemisphere, and even these birds migrate south for half the year during the non-breeding season. Eight species that breed on the Arctic tundra migrate to New Zealand during the northern winter, joining four endemic plovers here.

Wrybills number fewer than 5000 birds, and have a distinctive migration pattern within New Zealand. They breed early in the season on braided river beds and in the foothills of the Southern Alps. During the last weeks of December, when their breeding has finished, wrybills migrate north to tidal areas of coastal Northland, Thames, Manukau and the Coromandel. In early to mid-August they migrate south again to breed.

Wrybills are monogamous, and pairs share egg incubation and chick tending. The male uses his chest to bulldoze a nest hollow among greywacke pebbles, which the small, camouflaged eggs resemble perfectly. The eggs are very rich in yolk, which supports the chicks for the first few days after hatching; this is important as they are not fed by their parents.

Camouflage is a distinctive plover feature: the chicks are covered in sandy grey down, while adults are largely grey with a small amount of black and white which is not visible when the bird sits on the nest among the grey river stones. Adult wrybills have breeding and non-breeding plumage, and moult twice a year.

Black stilts are critically endangered, with only fifty or so birds remaining, including eleven breeding pairs.

BLACK STILT
Kaki *Himantopus novaezelandiae*

Stilts are a small but widespread group of birds and, remarkably, two of the world's eight species occur in New Zealand. Our endemic black stilt, the world's most critically endangered stilt, lives alongside the pied stilt, which is a subspecies of the black-winged stilt, the most successful and widespread stilt species.

Black stilts eat a range of aquatic prey from snails and small fish to insect larvae. All stilts have exceptionally long, thin bills and bright pink legs. Their bills are needle-like, and their very long, thin legs have comparatively short toes with limited but very important webbing, adequate for them to swim. Black stilts have shorter, more robust bills and shorter legs than pied stilts. Other stilts have varying amounts of black and white feathers, but as its name suggests the black stilt is pure black.

However, there are many pied and black stilt hybrids, known as smudgies. This hybridisation is threatening the survival of the black stilts, and is also creating a distinct New Zealand pied stilt that has more black on its back and shoulders. The hybrids occur because black stilts are territorially more aggressive than pied stilts, and female pied stilts often choose these dominant black stilts as mates. Because of the shortage of female black stilts, the males accept these pied mates.

Both black and pied stilts have a very elegant courtship. Standing in water, the female solicits by holding her body in a rigid horizontal posture, stretching her head and neck low and forward. The male responds by repeatedly dipping his bill in the water, shaking it and preening, before he mounts her back. After mating, she raises her neck and they cross bills as he steps off her, places one of his wings across her back and holds the other outstretched, and they remain like that briefly.

Black stilts begin breeding in August, when there is still snow on the hills in the Mackenzie Basin. They nest in solitary pairs at the edge of water, and defend their nests and young by attacking and dive-bombing predators. All these features make black stilts more vulnerable to predation than the colonial pied stilts that begin nesting later in the season on islands surrounded by water, lure predators away from their nests using guile and distraction, and fledge their chicks at 30 rather than 40 days.

🕊 *Early settlers in Canterbury called black-fronted terns plough birds or plough boys, after the large flocks which followed ploughs picking up grubs and worms.*

BLACK-FRONTED TERN
Sterna albostriata

Black-fronted terns are unusual endemic terns that breed inland on South Island braided rivers and lakes, and hawk for insects. Their winnowing flight and spectacular headlong plunge-dives are eye-catching.

Only two of the sixteen species of terns recorded in New Zealand are endemic: white-fronted terns are coastal inhabitants, while black-fronted terns spend the summer inland in the South Island, east of the Southern Alps, and in winter disperse to coastal estuaries and shores. Wintering birds cross Cook Strait to Wellington, occasionally making it as far north as Auckland, but most birds remain in the South Island.

During winter black-fronted terns feed at sea, mostly on plankton. They hunt on the wing in loose flocks of a hundred or more birds, and compared to marine tern species they beat, bank, hover and circle lower, on tighter, more varied transects. When feeding inland they dip to the water surface to pick off prey such as emerging aquatic insects and small fish, and in spring they revel in the mayfly hatch in snow-fed rivers. They hawk insects from the air, pluck them off vegetation or pick up worms and larvae from freshly turned soil.

Most tern species return each year to breed at the same nest site, but black-fronted terns breed on braided rivers which constantly change. Gravel bars, which are a favourite breeding site, often change after spring floods, so black-fronted terns return to their old colony, find their previous mate and then select a new nest site.

Despite their small size and slender build, black-fronted terns are fearless in defence of their nest. Birds will join together to mob predators around the colony, dive-bombing humans, gulls or harriers, and making angry, grating calls.

However, courage at the nest hasn't been enough to halt a significant decline in numbers, to fewer than 5000 birds. In fact, their habit of choosing a new nest site each year and their ability to adapt to disturbances such as floods mean black-fronted terns are equally likely to abandon their nest when disturbed by people. Other hazards facing the black-fronted tern population and their river homes include hydro-electricity schemes, pasture development, irrigation, encroaching lupins, broom and gorse, and predators such as cats, mustelids and hedgehogs.

The distinctive mallard call, a loud quaek-quaek-quak-quak-quak-qua, *is made only by the female. The male makes a soft, conversational, nasal* rhaeb *that he repeats frequently when swimming.*

MALLARD DUCK
Anas platyrhynchos

Mallards are the most widespread and recognised dabbling duck, forming large, noisy flocks on bodies of water as small as a puddle or as large as a lake. They originally occurred in the temperate northern hemisphere, through Europe, Asia and North America.

Dabbling ducks are the largest tribe of waterfowl, numbering 57 species. They feed on the surface of the water, or up-end to dabble just below the surface. Dabbling ducks are very widespread, and are found on all continents and on islands around the world.

The mallard is the only dabbling duck to have been domesticated in China or South-East Asia, about 5000 years ago. It has since been domesticated and selectively bred in parts of Europe to produce familiar breeds such as Aylesbury and Khaki Campbell. There are twelve common varieties of domestic mallard, bred for egg production and meat.

A few mallards were introduced into New Zealand in 1867, but failed to establish. Further breeding and liberations of British stock sourced from Australia were made between 1890 and 1918, mostly in Otago and Southland, and some small populations became established. During the 1930s and 1940s North American mallards were included in an intensive breeding and liberation programme that went on until the 1960s. Finally, mallards became New Zealand's most numerous and widespread waterfowl; there are now about three million birds, down from a high of five million in the early 1980s, and they are found on many offshore and outlying islands. Mallards have interbred so widely with native grey ducks (see page 134) that most ducks are now probably of hybrid ancestry, and can be legally shot during the hunting season.

Female mallards are cryptic brown in colour, as are males during their moult, when they are said to be in 'eclipse' plumage. During the breeding season, however, male mallards are brightly coloured, each with a bright yellow beak, metallic green head, white neck ring and vivid orange legs. Their courtship display is a series of complex movements designed to show their plumage to best advantage.

As well as dabbling in the water for food, mallards eat seeds from the water surface or nearby plants, aquatic arthropods and snails, crops such as peas and beans, and graze on grass and clover.

Until the mid 1960s, when the closely related, introduced mallard became dominant, grey ducks comprised about ninety-five percent of New Zealand's dabbling duck population; today it's closer to ten percent.

GREY DUCK
Parera *Anas superciliosa*

Grey ducks are very typical dabbling ducks, with comb-like lamellae on the inside of their bill that they use to sieve seeds and small invertebrates from the water. Grey ducks are the local native population of the Pacific black duck, which also occurs in Australia, New Guinea, Indonesia and on some Pacific islands.

Although grey ducks are still widespread, they are uncommon and most likely to live in remote, undisturbed areas such as forested streams and lakes; it is the introduced mallard that is the common duck on farms and in cities (see page 132). Pure grey ducks are cryptic brown, much like female mallards, but have distinctive pale stripes above and below their eyes. They also have a large rectangular speculum of metallic green on their dark brown wings, whereas mallards have a metallic blue speculum. Mallards and grey ducks interbreed, producing hybrids in which mallard characteristics such as orange legs, curly tails and a bluish speculum dominate. The resulting hybrids dominate and out-compete pure grey ducks in modified environments. Pure grey ducks also lay fewer eggs than mallards, and as they are easier to decoy in they are shot in disproportionate numbers during the hunting season.

When breeding, the female grey duck selects a nest site that may be up to 2 kilometres away from where she and her mate have their feeding territory. The down-filled nest is on the ground, in dense cover such as grass or sedges, and occasionally in a hole in a tree. After she lays each egg, the female covers the eggs with down, then flies back to the feeding territory to join her mate, which may accompany her back to the nest site. The male abandons her once the 28-day incubation starts, during which time the female leaves the nest only briefly, once or twice a day. After hatching, as soon as the last chick is dry, the female leads her brood to water. At first the ducklings feed on aquatic snails and invertebrates, as they need calcium and protein to grow their bones and muscles. Later, however, they feed increasingly on the leaves and seeds of aquatic plants, and worms and caterpillars found on wet pasture.

🕊 *Blue ducks are also known as whio, from the distinctive whistling feeyo made by the male. The call can be heard above the roar of a mountain torrent and advertises the presence of the pair.*

BLUE DUCK
Whio *Hymenolaimus malacorhynchos*

Blue ducks are very unusual dabbling ducks: they live in fast-flowing mountain streams, are insectivorous and territorial, and maintain long-lasting pair bonds.

Only four species of duck live year-round on rivers, and blue ducks are so distinctive it's not clear whether they have close relationships with any of the other species. They are sometimes considered to be related to torrent ducks in South America on account of the distinctively marked chicks of both species; blue duck chicks have striking iridescent green, white and chestnut down, and share with torrent duck chicks a white eyebrow stripe that is divided above the eye by a dark vertical stripe.

Adult blue ducks have steel-grey plumage that merges perfectly with the blue-grey river boulders of the steep, rapid rivers where they live. Their bills are edged with a flexible black rubbery flange that protects them from abrasion on rocks during feeding. They feed in shallow white-water, facing upriver with their heads and necks submerged, sucking aquatic invertebrates such as caddis flies off the sheltered downstream faces of the rocks. In deeper water they can dive for up to twenty seconds. They feed at dawn and dusk, hiding during the day under riverbank vegetation or log jams, or standing motionless on rocks.

Both birds in a pair defend a home range along a kilometre or so of river. They feed only in parts of the range, which may be so large to isolate the female from neighbouring birds and to provide chicks with quieter areas in which to feed. Males fight fiercely when they meet. Such fights may be followed by mate swaps, although pair bonds are generally long lasting.

Blue duck chicks hatch with disproportionately large feet, and from a young age they can swim against swift currents, walk and run across fast-moving water, and jump and climb well, watched over by very attentive parents. Breeding adults moult before the ducklings fledge, and it is thought that this ensures that the adults can fly before the young challenge them for territory. If young birds aren't successful in challenging for a mate or a home range they squeeze in between the ranges of existing pairs, feeding furtively and waiting for opportunities.

After the breeding season Canada goose families stay together for the winter. They congregate in wary but noisy flocks, making a musical honk-ah-honk *call.*

CANADA GOOSE
Branta canadensis

There are fifteen species of true geese, all found in the northern hemisphere. They walk and run well and graze on land, and although they can feed in water they are less aquatic than ducks.

Canada geese come from North America. There are up to twelve subspecies of Canada goose, and the ones introduced to New Zealand in 1905 and again in 1920 are descended from the largest subspecies, *maxima*. Known as 'honkers', Canada geese are found in the northern and central United States from North Dakota to Arkansas, and have been introduced to Britain, Scandinavia and elsewhere in Europe.

Numbering about 40,000 birds, Canada geese are abundant in the South Island, in the dry east from Marlborough to North Otago, and on dry river flats in eastern Fiordland. After regular introductions in the 1970s they have established in the central North Island, Waikato and Wairarapa. In the South Island they breed near high-country lakes and rivers, and both adults and juveniles usually migrate east to coastal lagoons such as Lake Ellesmere for the autumn moult. They stay near the coast for the winter, and migrate to higher areas in spring to nest. Recently, however, some birds have remained inland, moulting near inland lakes and feeding on the increasing number of improved and irrigated pastures.

Geese are vegetarian, and as they have a short, simple gut and lack bacteria to digest cellulose they obtain their nutrients from cell juices after grinding down the cell walls of leaves and stems in the gizzard. They have to feed for long periods to get adequate nutrition, and plants pass through their gut so undigested that it is possible to identify plants to species level in their droppings.

Canada geese are expert at selecting grasses with high nutrient levels, especially spring grasses that are rich in carbohydrate and soluble protein. They can be a nuisance feeding on autumn-saved and spring grass and clover growth, and can cause considerable damage to lucerne, brassica, pea and grain crops.

Canada geese are game birds that can be legally shot between May and July, and are also culled when they are damaging crops.

The female paradise shelduck has a striking white head, and as she is the more vividly marked of the pair she is often wrongly thought to be the male. Her white head may help the male tell when she is in the dark nest.

PARADISE SHELDUCK
Putangitangi *Tadorna variegata*

Shelducks are a group of waterfowl that combine characteristics of ducks and geese. There are seven shelduck species; five, including our paradise shelduck, are considered to be terrestrial grazing birds which feed on plants, while two are estuary inhabitants eating mud-worms and snails.

Paradise shelducks occur only in New Zealand, and are now widely distributed on the mainland in hill country, wetlands and especially farmland. They were uncommon during the 1800s, restricted to the east and south of the South Island, but the development of pastures with exotic grass and farm ponds has caused a significant increase in their numbers. Their increase since about 1990 has been spectacular and they are now present on many golf courses and urban parks.

Paradise shelducks nest in tree cavities, holes in the ground or rock crevices. One pair of paradise shelducks was observed nesting on the top shelf of a wardrobe in an abandoned farmhouse; to reach her nest the female had to fly through a broken window, land, walk up the hall to another room, and then fly up through the slightly open door of the wardrobe.

Paradise shelducks have one brood a year, and after 30 to 35 days' incubation the clutch of about nine eggs all hatches together. Although the nest may be in a forest tree 25 metres above the ground, the newly hatched chicks confidently jump out, tumble and bounce on landing, and then follow their mother up to a kilometre to open water. Young paradise shelducks are independent, but nevertheless have a strong attachment to their mother. This bond develops while the chick is developing in the egg, in response to calls, and the young always respond rapidly to that call, as well as following their mother.

On farmland, large broods of ducklings are a common sight, but on natural waterways a pair of paradise shelducks may have trouble raising one or two chicks to maturity, as it's difficult to protect an entire brood from underwater predators such as eels. When threatened the parents perform a distraction display, feigning injury to draw predators away from the chicks.

During December to February, well after breeding, all birds leave their territories to moult in large flocks at traditional sites such as tarns or ponds.

White-faced herons in flight have a distinctive silhouette; with their head and neck curled back they beat their broad wings slowly and deeply, and are capable of flying long distances.

WHITE-FACED HERON
Ardea novaehollandiae

White-faced herons arrived from Australia and established in New Zealand during the 1940s and 1950s. Like the sixty-one other species of heron found worldwide, they have long necks, bills, legs and toes.

White-faced herons are highly specialised predators that feed on a wide range of prey. They usually stalk live prey on land or as they wade in shallow water, or stand and wait for prey to appear. They also use their feet to stir mud in the bottom of ponds, follow stock as cattle egrets do, and forage on the rocky coast like reef herons. They can focus their eyes down the length of their bills to spot their target, and the neck and bill are well designed for catching food with a single rapid thrust. The neck vertebrae elongate so the neck unfolds like a hinge, and their sharp bills are used to grab or impale the target. White-faced herons prey on eels, frogs, insects, lizards, small mammals and even small birds.

They are highly mobile birds that move significant distances each day and during the course of a year. White-faced herons spend much of the non-feeding part of their day at their roost, resting and preening. They have special 'powder down' feathers on their flanks that provide absorbent dust used to clean slime and dirt off their bills.

Although they often feed together, white-faced herons don't breed in colonies as other herons do. During the breeding season these herons develop luxuriously long, textured plumes on their back, and males choose display sites high in a tree such as a pine or macrocarpa. A female chooses a male by entering his display ground and withstanding attempts to be driven away, and courtship and pair maintenance continue after the pair bond has been formed.

The display ground usually becomes the nesting territory, and the male gathers twigs and branches which the female builds into a bulky platform. Both birds incubate the three to five typically heron-blue eggs and feed the young. The chicks are helpless when they hatch but develop quickly, especially their legs, and within a week or two they can scramble in and out of the nest.

🕊 *In flight, mute swan wings make a loud singing or throbbing with each wing beat, a sound that Tchaikovsky captured beautifully in Swan Lake. The string section's fast flutter in the finale of the ballet is a perfect rendition of a flock of mute swans in flight.*

MUTE SWAN
Cygnus olor

Four species of pure white swans, including mute swans, originated in the northern hemisphere, while another three swan species, all with some black feathers, are found south of the equator.

Mute swans are heavily built, and at around 16 kilograms are the largest swan and one of the world's heaviest flying birds. To be able to fly, birds have very light bones; interestingly, a similar-sized mammal would weigh four times as much. They have a laborious take-off, running across the water and using strong flaps of their wings to get airborne. They are strong fliers, with a 2 metre wingspan, but they are so heavy they have to land on water. They have short legs, and on land have a clumsy, waddling gait.

In the northern hemisphere some populations migrate to breed. The natural range of mute swans is northern Europe, and because of their value as ornamental and luxury birds they became semi-domesticated. They were introduced to New Zealand from the United Kingdom in 1866, and maintain a tenuous hold here; about twenty mute swans survive in Hawke's Bay, and a further 80 or so birds live near Lake Ellesmere's Hart Creek and on nearby coastal lakes in Canterbury.

Mute swans are not as silent as their name suggests; however, their calls are not often heard, apart from their aggressive call which is a mean, snake-like hissing. Breeding mute swans can be very threatening, raising their wings like sails and arching their head and neck over their back.

During the breeding season males defend territories, chasing off intruding neighbours with wing-splashing rushes and slides across the water. They usually nest at the edge of lakes on a large mound of vegetation such as raupo, flax and reeds, laying their eggs in a shallow bowl lined with a few feathers. The female incubates the eggs alone, but both parents rear the chicks.

Outside the breeding season mute swans are usually found in small flocks comprising families, pairs and immature non-breeders. Mute swans feed in shallow water, using their long necks to reach submerged weeds. They also take frogs, fish and insects, pluck overhanging willow leaves and graze on clover and grass.

Black swans make a clear, musical, bugling contact call both in flight and on the water.

BLACK SWAN
Cygnus atratus

The black swan is one of Australia's best-known birds, and is the state bird of Western Australia. Black swans appear all black until in flight, when they reveal white primary feathers on their wings.

They naturally occur in mainland Australia, Tasmania and New Guinea. They were also native to New Zealand, but were exterminated by the first Polynesian settlers on the mainland and on the Chatham Islands. Coincidental with their reintroduction to New Zealand as a game bird in the 1860s black swans recolonised naturally, and were later taken back to the Chatham Islands. By the 1880s black swans were well established and widespread.

They are often nomadic, seeking out large areas of shallow water containing aquatic vegetation such as lakes, estuaries and flooded pastures. When they are moulting and therefore flightless, they prefer large lagoons near the coast, where they can safely remain a great distance from the shore. Black swans feed in shallow water on aquatic weeds, and with their long necks can reach deeper than ducks. They also feed extensively on lakeside pastures, where their droppings can cause fouling.

Black swans can occur in spectacular breeding concentrations; before the *Wahine* storm destroyed the *Ruppia* weed-beds in Lake Ellesmere in 1968 up to 70,000 birds were recorded in just one colony. Today, this is about the number of black swans found throughout New Zealand.

The breeding season is very long, and in the thermal Rotorua Lakes they can nest throughout winter. The nest is a shallow bowl lined with some down, on top of a huge mound of raupo leaves and flax. Both parents share incubation during the day, although the female usually incubates at night. The greenish-white eggs may become stained, as they are covered with damp vegetation when the nest is left unattended. Within a day of hatching, both parents lead the cygnets to water. In large breeding colonies, cygnets may form large crèches of up to 40 birds, guarded by a few adults. Immature swans have greyer plumage than adult birds in their first year, and retain a black tip on their otherwise white wing feathers for two to three years until they reach full adulthood.

Pukeko are one of our most successful and iconic native birds. Their distinctive colours are a familiar sight in many places, including median strips on busy Auckland motorways.

PUKEKO
Porphyrio melanotus

Rails are a widespread group of more than 130 species found on all continents except Antarctica, on almost all island groups, and in any habitat except deserts. They've been successful because they're opportunistic omnivores that eat a wide variety of food, they can fly, and they can also swim if they settle on water — all features which help them to disperse and survive.

Pukeko and flightless takahe (see page 68) are both grouped with gallinules and crakes, and classified in the genus *Porphyrio*, named for the Greek word for purple. Pukeko are one of about six similar species of purple swamp-hens, which range through southern Europe, Africa, Asia and the western Pacific. Differing in size, colour and social behaviour from the other species, pukeko also occur in Australia.

Pukeko swim well, often perch in trees, and use their long, splayed toes to walk over mud and floating vegetation. They feed on a wide range of plants, including cultivated crops, invertebrates, frogs, fish, small birds and eggs, mice and carrion, as well as artificial food such as bread, chocolate and dog food.

Elsewhere, the purple swamp-hen is monogamous and nests solitarily, but in New Zealand pukeko have much more complex and interesting social behaviour. Nesting areas are often limited, so pukeko occur in stable, communal groups of up to twelve related individuals. The group usually includes two to five breeding males, one or two breeding females, and several non-breeding helpers, often the previous year's young. Mating within the group is promiscuous, and includes incestuous and homosexual couplings. Only the dominant females breed and lay in a communal nest that may contain up to 25 eggs, although only up to eight chicks usually survive to be reared by the whole group. If food is plentiful the group may raise three clutches a year, the first chicks of the season helping raise the later chicks. Pukeko are very aware of predators and often defend their nests or young as a group, and their co-operative social and breeding behaviour has probably ensured their success.

🕊 *The banded rail bill is so big and strong that a female can carry her own eggs with it. If she's disturbed at the nest she'll move her eggs, one by one, to a new site.*

BANDED RAIL
Gallirallus philippensis

Banded rails are placed with weka and the Lord Howe woodhen in a group called *Gallirallus*, or the bar-winged rails. Native to New Zealand, banded rails are also widespread in Australia, Indonesia, the Philippines and islands of the southwest Pacific.

They were once widespread, but on the mainland they are now largely confined to mangroves and salt marshes with a regular supply of fresh water. On offshore islands such as Great Barrier and the Poor Knights they occur in damp grassland, scrub and forest, where they nest in tree hollows, under logs or under thick grass.

Banded rails can fly, and are smaller and slimmer than weka (see page 58). They have more intricately marked plumage with narrow black-and-white barred underparts, bold white eyebrows and chestnut eye stripes. They're extremely secretive, but usually give their presence away on hot, sunny days with a screech that sounds like a rusty gate. In the mangroves of north Auckland they can be seen foraging at low tide in the vegetated margins, on mud and among tall grass and reeds. They usually feed alone, probing and pecking in mud, shallow water, among leaf litter and even on pasture. They'll often peck at encrusting organisms growing on mangrove trunks. They have a robust beak which they use to grab large food items, retreating under cover to feed. They also use the bill to stab eggs and crush fish and snails before swallowing them.

Like most rails, banded rail chicks leave the nest within hours of hatching, and within a week are foraging for themselves. Chicks are frequently pecked and chased by their own parents; when being fed by a parent they usually hide between the adult's legs to avoid being pecked. Late in the breeding season adults frequently disrupt groups of chicks, rushing in and scattering them. Five to six weeks after hatching chicks are forcibly evicted from their parents' territory; although they are reluctant fliers, with enough provocation the chicks will eventually fly away.

Banded rails are not present on the Chatham Islands, which used to have their own flightless rail. Only one Dieffenbach's rail was ever seen and collected by Europeans, before cats and rats caused their extinction.

Coots spend much of their time on the water, and are frequently mistaken for ducks.

AUSTRALIAN COOT
Fulica atra

Coots are a group of rails with large lobed toes for swimming; this contrasts with the gallinules such as pukeko which have long, slender toes to walk on floating vegetation. The Australian coot is a native subspecies of the Eurasian coot, which occurs in Australia, New Guinea, Southeast Asia, India, North Africa and Europe.

The Australian coot was a rare vagrant here until the 1950s. Then they started to breed at Lake Hayes in 1958, joining two other Australian colonists, white-faced herons and royal spoonbills, which also became New Zealand residents around that time. Coots have greatly expanded their range since then and are now common in Otago, Canterbury and much of the North Island.

Australian coots have white bills and shields, and slate-grey bodies that often appear black on the water. Unusually for rails they prefer large, open areas of water for feeding and dense vegetation for nesting; reed-lined lakes are a favoured place, although they're also found in ponds and slow rivers. They dive frequently to feed on plants, but will sometimes up-end. If disturbed they prefer to run away across water, rather than fly, but they can fly strongly on broad, round wings, with their long legs trailing; this is also a characteristic of other flighted rails. On some city ponds they can become tame enough to feed along with ducks on bread and grain. Like other rails they moult all their flight feathers at once, and spend their annual flightless period in groups on lakes, far from the shore.

Coots build their nests on floating platforms of reed stems, or on partially submerged branches under the cover of willows. The nests often have an entrance ramp, and occasionally a woven hood. The coots lay five to seven creamy-white, spotted eggs, which are incubated by both sexes for 22 days. Coot chicks have cream bills and are covered in dark brown down, except on their heads where the down is tipped in reddish orange. Coots commonly renested two or three times in a breeding season while they were establishing in New Zealand, but both clutch size and the number of nestings have reduced as their population has increased.

Adult fernbirds usually stay close to their home territory, but young birds may travel great distances.

FERNBIRD
Matata *Bowdleria punctata*

Fernbirds belong to the Old World warbler family, which despite the name does not contain birds such as grey warblers. There are nearly four hundred species of Old World warbler, mostly found in Eurasia and Africa, although a few species do occur in the New World.

Old World warblers are generally small, brownish birds that tend to hide in dense vegetation, appearing only briefly before disappearing again in search of invertebrates. They have fine, narrowly pointed bills and strong feet well suited for perching and for lifting up leaves. Some species, including New Zealand's endemic fernbirds, have long tails that counterbalance the body as birds thread their way through thick foliage, tirelessly searching leaves and branches for insects. Fernbirds share their distinctive fern-like tails with other unusual Old World warblers: Madagascar's two species of emutails and the grass bird of southern Africa. Their tails appear ragged and spiky because the feather barbs are not joined together.

Although they are not especially wary, fernbirds are secretive, and creep mouse-like through the stems of swamp or scrub vegetation. When they fly it's a laboured fluttering, with their tail hanging down behind.

Many warblers are great songsters, but in this respect fernbirds are very different. Their main call is a sharp mechanical *uu-tick*. Although males sometimes make this call on their own, it is more usually an antiphonal call: an alternating duet between both members of the pair, in which the male calls a brief *uu* and the female responds instantaneously with the corresponding *tick*. Rarely, fernbirds make a melodic warble, and they sometimes also produce a quiet series of rapid metallic clicks.

There are five subspecies of the New Zealand fernbird: North Island, South Island, Stewart Island, Codfish Island and Snares Island. The extinct Chatham Island fernbird was a separate, more colourful species.

Fernbirds weave feather-lined nests from rushes and grasses and suspend them about a metre above the ground between rush or tussock stems. They lay two to four eggs that hatch after a sixteen-day incubation by both parents. The chicks are independent five weeks after hatching, and a pair of fernbirds may renest two or three times in a breeding season.

5

Sea and shore

Tube-nosed seabirds have the widest range of body mass of any order of birds. Great albatrosses weigh nearly 10 kilograms, while storm petrels weigh just 20 grams.

WANDERING ALBATROSS
Diomedea exulans

The great albatrosses are distinguished from other tube-nosed seabirds by their huge size, 3 metre wingspans, and the position of their external tubular nostrils, which lie on each side of the bill near the base, rather than being fused on top of the bill.

The great albatrosses comprise the royal and wandering groups, which are variously regarded by taxonomists as being from two to seven species. Two of the five kinds of wandering albatross breed in the New Zealand region: about 8000 pairs of Gibson's wanderers breed on the Auckland Islands, and 9000 pairs of Antipodean wanderers breed on the Antipodes and Campbell islands. The remaining wandering albatrosses breed on subantarctic islands in the Indian, Atlantic and Pacific oceans

Albatrosses are renowned for the length of their wings, and have much longer forearm bones relative to hand-bone length than other tube-nosed seabirds. Between 25 and 34 secondary wing feathers attach to the albatross's forearm, compared to just ten or twelve feathers in the much smaller storm petrels, and a special tendon locks the extended wing into position. These features create a wing that is a very efficient aerofoil, and its high aspect-ratio of length to width allows fast forward gliding with a very low sinking rate. This efficient gliding allows albatrosses to make rapid long-distance flights, traversing vast tracts of windswept Southern Ocean between Antarctica and the southern tips of South America, Africa, Australia and New Zealand.

Male birds are heavier than females and have longer wings, so they can feed in stormier conditions. Wandering albatrosses usually seize fish, squid and crustaceans from the sea surface, often feeding at night when their prey rises to the surface. They can effortlessly follow ships at sea for hours with barely a wing beat. Wandering albatrosses have broad diets, and will scavenge offal thrown overboard as well as the bait on longlines set behind fishing boats, a habit which causes the drowning of many birds each year. Nineteenth-century sailors caught and ate albatrosses, used their wing bones as pipes, and turned their feet into tobacco pouches.

Juvenile wandering albatrosses have brown bodies and white faces and throats. As they get older they become increasingly white, although they retain varying amounts of brown on their backs.

The name albatross comes from the Portuguese alcatraz, and was originally used for any large seabird. In turn it is apparently derived from the earlier Arabic term for pelican, al cadous.

ROYAL ALBATROSS
Toroa *Diomedea epomophora*

Royal albatrosses have elaborate courtship rituals that involve bowing, bill-fencing with loud clattering, and dancing with outstretched wings. Both partners 'skycall', throwing their heads back with their beaks pointing skywards and braying loudly. Up to six pairs of different ages may take part in display ceremonies to form pair bonds which can last for life.

Royal albatrosses are long-lived birds, reaching 30 years on average, although one female, known as 'Grandma', was still breeding in her 60s. Albatrosses are slow breeders; although capable of breeding at six years of age, most start several years after that, even as late as fifteen years. Young birds make short visits to the breeding grounds at first, late in the season, spending increasing time ashore in subsequent breeding seasons as they court prospective mates. Once a pair has established they usually remain together until one partner dies, with a rare 'divorce' occurring only after several breeding failures. Divorce is costly: it reduces a bird's lifetime reproductive success by 10 to 20 percent.

Royal albatrosses lay a single, large, white egg, and during the 79-day incubation period both birds take turns, in shifts lasting several days. For the first four to five weeks after the chick hatches the parents initially brood and then guard it. Both parents then forage at sea, returning to land regularly to feed the chick. Royal albatross chicks take eleven months to fully develop and take their first flight; wandering albatross chicks (see page 158) take twelve months. This extremely long chick-rearing period means these albatrosses can only breed every second year, as once breeding is complete birds must moult before they can breed again.

Southern royal albatrosses breed on Campbell Island and the Auckland Islands, while northern royal albatrosses breed on the Sisters and Forty Fours Island in the Chatham group. A small population of northern royals breeds on the mainland, at Taiaroa Head near Dunedin, but interestingly fossil evidence has not yet been found of any of the great albatrosses or smaller mollymawks breeding on the New Zealand mainland in pre-human times. Non-breeding birds disperse downwind throughout the Southern Ocean, ranging mainly east of New Zealand to both coasts of South America.

The name mollymawk comes from the Dutch malle mok *meaning 'stupid gull'; it was originally given to the northern hemisphere fulmar prion.*

CAMPBELL MOLLYMAWK
Thalassarche impavida

Campbell mollymawks are also known as New Zealand black-browed mollymawks, and breed only on subantarctic Campbell Island. Mollymawks are small to medium-sized albatrosses, and are currently subject to intense taxonomic debate, with between five and eleven species identified.

Mollymawks are large, long-winged seabirds, and are clearly separated from the great albatrosses by their smaller size, dark tail and the dark 'bridge' linking the upper wings across their back. All mollymawks have a smudged mascara-like area around their eyes, called a loral patch, and a white crescent on the lower rear eye-ring. Campbell mollymawks and the other very similar black-browed mollymawks have extensive, prominent loral patches, and can only be distinguished at close range. Campbell mollymawks have a more extensive black eyebrow, straw-coloured eyes and more black on their underwings, while black-browed mollymawks have dark eyes and cleaner white underwings.

More than three million black-browed mollymawks breed on islands throughout the subantarctic, mostly on the Falklands, with small numbers breeding in the New Zealand region on the Snares and Antipodes islands. There are only 25,000 pairs of Campbell mollymawks, restricted to breeding on Campbell Island and the tiny nearby islet of Jeanette Marie.

Mollymawks breed in dense colonies, and the single egg is laid on top of a small nest pedestal built from soil and vegetation. Pairs carry out elaborate bonding displays, and baa, wail, croak and cackle, as well as bill-snap.

After breeding, Campbell mollymawks disperse to subantarctic waters in the south Pacific, Tasman Sea and the Ross Sea. They feed on fish, krill and some squid and jellyfish, caught by surface seizing, diving or plunging. They follow boats and whales, and readily consort in large groups with other feeding seabirds, even scavenging and stealing prey from other birds.

Populations of both black-browed and Campbell mollymawks have been falling. Not only have food stocks declined, but the birds are caught as by-catch by trawlers and longline fishing boats, with black-browed mollymawk species among the most frequently killed.

The courtship displays of white-capped mollymawks include loud braying and cackling noises.

WHITE-CAPPED MOLLYMAWK
Thalassarche steadi

White-capped mollymawks are a medium-sized seabird, and belong to a group of four species collectively known as shy mollymawks. Two of the four shy mollymawk species are endemic to New Zealand.

Shy mollymawks have a narrow, dark outline to the underwing and a small, distinctive thumbprint in the 'armpit' at the base of the wing's leading edge. All species have white bellies, chests and rumps, with varying amounts of grey on their heads.

White-capped mollymawks are the largest mollymawk, and as their name suggests they have very white heads. Their bills are a pale bluish horn colour with a pale yellow tip. The smaller Tasmanian mollymawk also has a white-capped head and is difficult to distinguish from the white-capped mollymawk.

White-capped mollymawks breed on three islands in the Auckland Islands group, and also on Bollons Island in the Antipodes. The total breeding population numbers about 80,000 pairs, 65,000 of those on Disappointment Island. On the main Auckland Island, wild pigs and cats have had significant impacts on the small remaining breeding colonies. White-capped mollymawks form large colonies on vegetated steep slopes or wide ledges. Pairs build a bowl-shaped pillar from dried mud, feathers, guano and vegetation in which to lay their single white egg. All albatrosses and mollymawks feed their young by forcibly regurgitating a mixture of oil and stomach contents into a trough in their lower mandible while their bills are open. The chick puts its bill at a right angle to its parent's lower bill and takes the food directly into its own trough.

White-capped mollymawks eat fish and squid, as well as barnacles and crustaceans, which they usually take at the surface. They feed in large groups with other albatrosses and seabird species, and often gather near whales and boats. As a result of their habit of following boats, large numbers were being caught in squid trawl wires, but a change in fishing practice has seen this death toll drop. A smaller number of white-capped mollymawks are also caught on longlines.

Outside the breeding season white-capped mollymawks disperse west into the Southern Ocean, as far as the western side of South Africa.

After breeding at the Bounties, Salvin's mollymawks mainly disperse east to South America, where they are common off the coast of Chile and southern Peru.

SALVIN'S MOLLYMAWK
Thalassarche salvini

Salvin's mollymawks belong to the shy mollymawk group of tube-nosed seabirds, and have an ill-defined and variable white cap on their forehead and forecrown. Their face has a typical 'unhappy frown', formed by their black, triangular loral patch, and their bill is a dusky olive-brown with a slightly yellow culmen and lower mandible with a dark smudge at the tip.

About 99 percent of the world population of Salvin's mollymawks breed on the Bounties and the Snares islands. It seems their numbers may have been declining, although differences in techniques during the occasional surveys may be partially responsible for this difference in numbers. In 1978 there were an estimated 76,500 pairs on the Bounties, compared to 30,750 pairs counted during the 1990s. A more recent survey in 2005 suggested a further drop of 14 percent on just one island in the group. Global warming, extreme weather events at the mollymawk's exposed breeding grounds, increases in breeding seal numbers and changes in food availability may account for this decline, as Salvin's mollymawks are not commonly caught in the longline or trawl fisheries.

Salvin's mollymawks breed in open colonies on level ground, building low, chimneypot-style nests of mud, guano, feathers and rock chips. The single white egg has reddish-brown spots at the broad end, and hatches after a 68- to 75-day incubation. Both sexes incubate the egg and feed the young. As the islands they breed on are so remote and little visited, it's not known how long it takes for the chicks to fledge.

The Bounty Islands, twenty small, low islands totalling just 135 hectares, are the smooth granite tips of the submerged Bounty Platform, the last vestiges of a disappearing continent. The largest island, Depot, is just 800 metres long, with its highest point only 88 metres above sea level; during storms the entire island is engulfed in spray. These bare rock outcrops have virtually no soil, and although the higher islands are covered in highly polished guano, rain and sea spray wash even that off the lower islands. However, the islands are crowded with life, such as fur seals, fulmar prions and erect-crested penguins, as well as Salvin's mollymawks.

Despite their large size and aggressive behaviour around carcasses, northern giant petrels are very timid around humans when breeding.

GIANT PETREL
Macronectes halli

The two species of giant petrel, northern and southern, are fearless and powerful predators and scavengers. Almost the size of a small albatross, but with a stouter body and smaller wings, giant petrels are the largest members of the Fulmarine petrel group.

All of the Fulmarine petrels have robust bills with prominent, joined nasal tubes rising from their base. Giant petrels are unique among tube-nosed seabirds in being able to feed on land; on the ground they can stand and support themselves on upright shanks, whereas most other petrels and shearwaters rest on their heels and outstretched shanks.

Male giant petrels are larger and more robust than the females, and do much of the killing and feeding on dead birds and marine mammals. The smaller females eat squid, fish and crustaceans taken at the sea surface.

Both species of giant petrel occur in New Zealand waters at different times of the year, and are difficult to tell apart. Both species have a massive, horn-coloured bill, but the southern giant petrel has a greenish bill tip, while the northern species has a pinkish bill tip. About 10 percent of southern giant petrels are white. In both species, juveniles have dark irises and adults pale ones.

Both species are circumpolar and nest in colonies among tussocks near cliffs on the windward side of subantarctic islands. The northern giant petrel is regarded as uncommon throughout its range, and breeds only on the Sisters and Forty Fours in the Chathams; an island in Port Pegasus, Stewart Island; and the Antipodes, Auckland Islands and Campbell Island.

Giant petrels have a keen sense of smell. They were nicknamed 'nellies' or 'stinkers' by sealers and whalers, from their habit of following ships to scavenge offal and scavenging in large groups at whaling stations and freezing-works outflows.

Giant petrels noisily maintain their pecking order at carcasses with threats and intimidatory displays. With outstretched wings, tail fanned and tilted upwards, and neck feathers ruffled, the bird sways its head from wing to wing, making a neighing cry. They appear pterodactyl-like as they make similar territorial displays in the air, stalling in mid-air and swaying their heads. At the nest, adults and chicks defend themselves by bill-snapping and squirting an oily slurry of stomach contents at intruders.

Unusually among seabirds, brown skuas at the Chatham Islands sometimes form breeding trios of a female and two unrelated males.

BROWN SKUA
Catharacta skua

Skuas are aggressive, predatory seabirds allied to gulls. There are five big, burly southern hemisphere species, which have a lumbering flight, and three smaller species, known as jaegars, which have a more dashing flight. Jaegars breed in the Arctic and winter at sea in the southern hemisphere.

Around 2000 brown skuas breed in the New Zealand region. They are common on southern outlying islands such as Campbell, Auckland and the Chathams, with a few birds breeding on Stewart Island and in Fiordland. Brown skuas are year-round residents of the Chatham Islands, while birds from more southern colonies show limited dispersal and short-distance migrations. Most spend the winter at sea, and may be seen around the coast of the main islands, especially after winter storms.

Brown skuas are long-lived and monogamous for life, although about 10 percent of pairs 'divorce' each year, usually following several failed breeding seasons. The larger male skuas defend the nest fiercely by dive-bombing intruders, including humans, striking them hard on the head with their knuckles. Territorial displays include a conspicuous heraldic display in which a bird holds its wings stiffly upwards to display its white wing patches, and extends its head and neck forward, uttering a long *charr-charr-charr* call. Skuas don't usually breed until they are eight years old, and non-breeding birds may form 'clubs' until breeding territories become available.

Skuas have gull-like feet with prominent, sharp claws, and hard, strongly hooked beaks adapted for tearing flesh. They feed by scavenging penguin eggs, and by killing penguin chicks and small burrowing seabirds. They also eat a wide range of fish and krill. During the breeding season they carry seabirds they have killed to middens near their nests, where they leave discarded heads, wings and legs in a scattered pile.

The related south polar skua breeds in Antarctica, and has one of the longest known migrations of any bird; a bird seen at Anvers Island in the Antarctic was recorded five months later in Greenland. South polar skuas have been seen closer to the South Pole than any other vertebrate apart from humans.

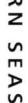

🕊 *The name cormorant comes from the Latin* corvus marinus, *meaning sea raven.*

CHATHAM ISLAND SHAG
Leucocarbo onslowi

There are up to thirty-nine species of birds variously called shags or cormorants, all of which are highly adapted for underwater hunting. They thrust through the water using their large, webbed feet for propulsion, hunting along the seabed for prey such as flatfish, squid and octopus.

Shags' bodies are streamlined and somewhat flattened beneath. Their necks are long and supple and they have broad, long, blunt wings, and powerful legs set far back on their bodies. They have denser bones than other flying birds, a noticeable absence of body fat and feathers that are not waterproof — all factors which reduce buoyancy and increase the efficiency of underwater pursuit. Lack of waterproof feathers means they can't stay submerged for long periods without leaving the water to dry out, although a large volume of blood allows them to store oxygen, and single dives may last up to four minutes. As an aid to hunting, the shape of the lens in the eye varies when the bird is underwater. Shags' bills have hugely distensible sides so they can swallow large prey, and they are such efficient hunters that they can usually meet their daily food needs in two fairly short diving sessions.

Chatham Island shags belong to a distinctive threesome of New Zealand marine shags collectively known as pink-footed shags. Chatham Island and Stewart Island shags are smaller and have more colourful facial skin than king shags living in the Marlborough Sounds. During the breeding season Chatham Island shags have striking nuptial adornments including a crest, red facial skin, fleshy orange growths above the bill and blue eye-rings, all of which fade outside the breeding season. Juveniles have brownish plumage, and adults have black-and-white plumage with an iridescent sheen.

In 2003 as few as 270 pairs of Chatham Island shags were recorded, making it the most threatened species of cormorant in the world. They occur in about ten colonies in the Chathams, with about half the birds breeding on the Star Keys. They usually feed offshore in deeper water, either alone or in small flocks, and outside the breeding season roost in small flocks of up to 50 birds. Chatham Island shags overlap in distribution with only one other shag species, the Pitt Island shag.

Red-billed gulls are highly gregarious, assembling in massive flocks year-round to breed, feed, roost and bathe.

RED-BILLED GULL
Tarapunga *Larus novaehollandiae*

Red-billed gulls are the most familiar and numerous gull of the New Zealand coast, recognisable by their bright red legs and habit of scavenging at beaches. Red-billed gulls are also found in Australia and New Caledonia, and are widespread on New Zealand's three main islands and many offshore islands.

All gulls are generally monogamous and pair for life. As the breeding season approaches birds assemble in large, dense colonies, frequently reclaiming their nest site from the previous year. The density of red-billed gull colonies depends on the local food supply; in temperate areas with high numbers of euphausiid krill available within a few kilometres, nests can be as close together as 1 metre, with pairs defending nesting territories little larger than the nest itself.

Males are very territorially aggressive. They have an impressive repertoire of aggressive and appeasement displays and calls, and although fights do sometimes break out, most behaviour is ritualised to avoid injury. Such territorial displays of strength by males also attract females, who typically approach bachelor males tentatively in a submissive, cowed posture. Once the male accepts the female, he feeds her as a prelude to mating and egg-laying.

Red-billed gulls lay two to three eggs, and the third egg is typically much smaller and a different colour to the others. This hatches much later than the others, and the runt chick is most likely to die if the food supply is limited. Chicks are mobile as soon as their down dries, although for a week or so after hatching they remain at or near the nest being brooded and tended by a parent. Later on, young birds often seek refuge in vegetation or other cover around the nest, where their speckled down serves as good camouflage as they crouch motionless. Chicks that trespass into neighbouring territories are fiercely attacked, and injury and even death can result.

After breeding red-billed gulls may disperse to offshore waters, often congregating at food-rich cold-water upwellings at the edge of the continental shelf. They usually settle at their night roost with full crops, which they digest at leisure as they rest.

Black-backed and red-billed gulls have benefited from human settlement, and have probably never been as abundant as they are now.

BLACK-BACKED GULL
Karoro *Larus dominicanus*

Piratical-looking southern black-backed gulls are the largest and most heavily built of New Zealand's gulls. Despite their stout build they are graceful in flight, switching easily from powerful forward flight to gliding and soaring. Their manoeuvrability serves them well as they fly on updrafts near cliffs. They are equally at home on the water surface, where their large webbed feet provide propulsion.

Black-backed gulls are familiar and widespread around New Zealand, as they are in other cool temperate parts of the southern hemisphere, where they are also known as Dominican or kelp gulls. Their expanding range includes the coasts of all the southern continents, including parts of Antarctica. In New Zealand, most black-backed gulls live at or near the coast, where they breed in large colonies, although they also live well inland, with some isolated pairs even breeding high in the Southern Alps on alpine tarns. With increasing urbanisation, black-backed gulls are favouring rooftops and buildings as nesting and roosting sites.

Gulls are supreme opportunists with a range of feeding habits, and southern black-backed gulls are no exception. Essentially a fish-eating species, they surface-plunge to take fish at sea, and smash open shellfish by carrying them to a great height and dropping them on hard surfaces such as roads, rocks or roofs. They scavenge food waste at dumps, and as a result their numbers have increased hugely with the spread of human habitation. However, with the move to recycling, incineration and buried landfills their numbers are falling again. Black-backed gulls living inland enjoy a wide range of natural foods, supplemented on farms with sheep afterbirths and lamb's tails. They also follow ploughs, taking earthworms and other soil invertebrates, and in autumn, after crops are harvested, they will even feed on stubble grain.

Black-backed gulls often prey on the chicks of other birds that share their breeding areas, with some adults specialising in killing chicks and feeding them to their own young. They also harass other birds such as white-fronted terns and red-billed gulls (see page 174) in a skua-like manner, forcing them to disgorge their food. At the nest, chicks jostle for food, pecking at the bright red spot near the tip of the bright yellow bill of the adult that serves as a target and begging stimulus.

🕊 *Caspian terns are long-lived, and once they reach adulthood it is not unusual for birds to survive to twenty or even thirty years old.*

CASPIAN TERN
Taranui *Hydroprogne caspia*

Caspian terns may be relatively recent colonists, as they weren't recorded in New Zealand until the mid-nineteenth century. They remained scarce until the 1930s, but have since increased in numbers.

Nearly as large as a black-backed gull, Caspian terns are more closely related to gulls than the smaller white-fronted terns are. They are less agile and streamlined than these small terns, graceful and familiar inhabitants of shorelines and beaches. White-fronted terns have small, pincer-like bills; Caspian tern bills are bright red and dagger-like, with a black tip. Caspian terns are strong fliers that can maintain a sustained, laboured hover with their head and bill facing down. They may plunge into the water from a height of 15 or so metres, to catch bottom-dwelling fish such as stargazers and small flounder. Although they will fully submerge, Caspian terns do not swim underwater. They also seize surface-swimming fish such as yellow-eyed mullet and piper. Their feet are webbed but small, and these birds seldom settle on the water for long.

Caspian terns were first studied in the Caspian Sea — hence their name — and have one of the most cosmopolitan distributions of any seabird. They breed in temperate areas on all continents except South America. In New Zealand they breed on both main islands, usually in coastal colonies numbering fewer than 100 pairs. Estuarine shell banks and sand spits are favoured colony sites. Single pairs or small groups also nest on sandy beaches at the entrance to harbours and estuaries, often associated with southern black-backed gull colonies (see page 176). However, as human activity and settlement increases around our coastline, undisturbed breeding sites are becoming increasingly scarce, and Caspian terns have been forced to move to less suitable areas.

Small numbers of Caspian terns breed inland, especially around Lake Rotorua and Canterbury riverbeds. Inland birds catch galaxiids, bullies, small eels and trout. Juvenile Caspian terns stand in shallow water and dip-feed for worms and small flounder.

Adult Australasian gannets have a distinct yellow head, and dark grey feet which are picked out with blue-yellow lines along the toes.

AUSTRALASIAN GANNET
Takapu *Morus serrator*

Notable for their dramatic plunge-diving and teeming breeding colonies, temperate members of the *Sulidae* family are known as gannets. Australasian gannets have heavy, streamlined bodies and long wings, and are capable of fast, sustained flight. The cutting edges of the bill are serrated for seizing fish, and the upper mandible, which curves down at the tip, can move upwards to accommodate large prey.

Australasian gannets forage in coastal inshore waters, characteristically in communal flocks that may contain hundreds of birds. Salvo after salvo of birds hurl themselves after fish, from heights of up to 15 metres. The initial dive may take a bird 1 to 2 metres underwater, and then it may dive deeper, propelled by its wings and feet. The impact of the dive is cushioned by inflatable air sacs between the skin and muscles of the lower neck and breast, and a solid, reinforced skull. Gannets lack exposed external nostrils, which are incompatible with diving, but they have binocular vision, which is important for three-dimensional perception.

Gannets usually nest in crowded colonies on predator-free offshore islands or remote coastal headlands such as Cape Kidnappers, surrounded by easily accessible feeding areas. There are 37 gannetries, containing more than 60,000 pairs of Australasian gannets, most of which are in New Zealand, with the remainder in southeast Australia. Unlike many other bird species, Australasian gannets have been increasing in number, by an average of 2.3 percent a year between the 1940s and 1980s.

Male gannets choose nest sites by reconnoitring from the air. Their small nest area within a large colony will be their only territory, but once they have selected a site they display and defend it against other gannets; territorial fights can be ferocious. The single egg is small compared to those of many other seabirds, and is incubated under the webs of the parents' feet. When food is plentiful the chick may fledge rapidly, leaving the nest in fewer than a hundred days. Fledglings go to sea unaccompanied, and the survival rate of young gannets is low. The brown-feathered, white-spotted juveniles disperse quickly to eastern and southern waters off Australia, and are not commonly seen around New Zealand. They return to breed three to seven years later.

During spring and summer Hutton's shearwaters feed in coastal waters, from Cook Strait to Otago.

HUTTON'S SHEARWATER
Puffinus huttoni

The surviving populations of Hutton's shearwaters that nest above 1500 metres altitude in subalpine grassland in the Seaward Kaikoura Range are the last significant burrowing seabird populations on mainland New Zealand. Their colonies are rich in plants, invertebrates and reptiles, and are living, functioning examples of how rich New Zealand ecosystems once were.

The importance of the shearwaters and petrels that once nested all over mainland New Zealand has only recently been realised and cannot be overstated. By sheer numbers alone, they were the most significant part of the avifauna. A substantial portion of nutrient flow through the terrestrial food chain came directly from the oceans, through the birds' guano. With their habit of nesting in burrows in large colonies, seabirds influenced the terrestrial environment more than any other vertebrate. As they burrowed they buried waste and turned over the ground, creating rich, aerated soils.

Shearwaters have long, slender bills and flat nasal tubes. About fifteen species live in New Zealand. There is one small and another large colony of Hutton's shearwaters remaining in the Seaward Kaikoura Ranges, numbering perhaps 100,000 pairs, which were discovered only in the 1960s. Hutton's shearwaters also bred in large colonies in the Inland Kaikouras, and had been harvested as muttonbirds during the 1800s.

It is impossible to know if Hutton's shearwaters were once even more widespread, as it is hard to tell their bones from those of fluttering shearwaters; indeed, there has been debate about whether Hutton's shearwaters should be considered a subspecies of the Manx shearwater, along with other similar and widespread black-and-white shearwaters.

In spring, when Hutton's shearwaters return from overwintering in Australian waters, the colony is often still covered in up to 2 metres of snow. The birds immediately locate the area over their buried burrow, and return each night to wait until the snow has melted enough for them to clean it out and lay their single egg.

Kea (see page 64) demonstrate their carnivorous tendencies by taking eggs and killing and eating Hutton's shearwater chicks, while predation by introduced stoats on both young and adults can be intense.

Mottled petrels are very vocal in the sky over their breeding colonies, making a rapid ti-ti-ti-ti or kek-kek-kek-kek.

MOTTLED PETREL
Korure *Pterodroma inexpectata*

Mottled petrels are one of about thirty species of gadfly petrels, all highly agile seabirds with long wings, and short, laterally compressed black bills that are strongly hooked at the tip. Mottled petrels are 'true' seabirds; they remain far from land except while they are nesting, and they have the most extensive range at sea of any bird.

They are nocturnal on land, arriving after dark and departing at or before first light, thus avoiding diurnal predators. Breeding colonies of mottled petrels, like all petrels, are found mostly on islands without mammalian predators. On land mottled petrels are clumsy and unable to take flight rapidly, and their only defence is to bite or spit stomach oils. Nestling petrels are especially vulnerable; the single chick is left on its own from about two days old, except when being fed, while its parents feed at sea, and for a week or two before fledging it spends much of the night outside the nest burrow, exercising its wings. When cats and rats are introduced, mottled petrel populations quickly plummet, often to extinction.

Two thousand years ago, before Polynesians and Pacific rats removed vast populations, the mottled petrel was one of the most abundant birds on the North and South islands. Now it's virtually extinct on the mainland, except for one tiny population on an islet in Lake Hauroko in Fiordland. The presence of mottled petrel feathers in rock wren nests in Fiordland suggests that a few birds may also still nest on steep cliffs around this coast. Today they breed on southern islands off the Fiordland and Stewart Island coasts, and on the Solander and Snares islands. Their current numbers are much lower than they once were, although mottled petrels are still regarded as a common seabird, with the Codfish Island colony alone numbering about two million birds. The effect of the loss of marine nutrients once delivered by the birds to the young soils of mainland New Zealand is incalculable.

Mottled petrels are seldom seen in New Zealand waters; during the breeding season they range into subantarctic waters as far as the pack ice, feeding at the ocean surface on lantern fish, small squid and crustaceans. Between March and June birds migrate to the subarctic waters of the North Pacific and Bering Sea.

While most petrels fly above the sea surface and over waves, diving petrels will fly into and right through a rising wave.

DIVING PETREL
Kuaka *Pelecanoides urinatrix*

Diving petrels are the southern hemisphere, tube-nosed seabird equivalent of auks, such as puffins, in the northern hemisphere. Although unrelated, little auks and diving petrels share the same whirring bumblebee-like flight, and their small wings, adapted for swimming underwater, are remarkably similar in bone structure.

Diving petrels have small, dumpy bodies, a stubby, hooked, black beak, and lavender-blue feet that are brighter during the breeding season. They fly rapidly, and are the most aquatic of all petrels. They swim penguin-like underwater, using their wings for propulsion and their short legs, set far back on their body, for steering. They chase prey such as euphausiid krill and small crustacea, mainly in the upper 10 metres of water, although they can dive to at least 60 metres. Emerging at the surface from a dive they scurry across the water with whirring wings to take off into the air.

There are four species of diving petrel. The most widespread is the common diving petrel, which has a circumpolar distribution. These birds used to breed on mainland New Zealand, and their bones are often found in laughing owl middens. They are vulnerable to predation by rats and cats, and decline where grazing mammals such as cattle compact the soil and trample their burrows. They burrow in peaty or rocky soils, and now breed in large colonies on many islands, from the Three Kings in the north to islets around Campbell Island in the south. Following the eradication of rats they should soon recolonise Campbell Island itself. They are sedentary birds, and feed in coastal waters all around New Zealand.

Slightly smaller South Georgian diving petrels also breed in New Zealand, with a tiny population of 50 or so pairs breeding in dunes on Codfish Island, near Stewart Island. This population is slowly recovering since weka and rats were eradicated. They feed further offshore than common diving petrels, on euphausiid krill and other crustacea. Along with common diving petrels, this species breeds on South Georgia Island in the South Atlantic, and numbers in the millions.

The generic name for diving petrels, *Pelecanoides*, comes from the pelican-like gular pouch below their bill. They store barely digested food in this pouch to feed to their chicks, rather than feeding them oily, pre-digested stomach contents as other petrels do.

🕊 *Fairy prions were once known as whale birds, as they are frequently found feeding in the same plankton-rich areas as whales and dolphins.*

FAIRY PRION
Titi wainui *Pachyptila turtur*

Prions are small seabirds, pale blue above and white below, with a prominent M-shaped mark across their upper wings, and a dark-tipped tail. Some use comb-like lamellae on the inside of their bills to filter zooplankton. Prions with fine bills peck prey such as krill and small fish, while prions with broad bills feed as they hydroplane across the surface of the sea. Prions congregate in areas of high plankton concentration, with vast flocks typically wheeling low over the sea.

There are about half a dozen prion species, all breeding in the Southern Ocean and rarely found elsewhere. Fairy prions are the smallest prion. They have a circumpolar distribution and are New Zealand's most common prion. More than a million pairs breed on offshore islands including the Chathams, Snares, Antipodes and Macquarie islands, islands in Cook and Foveaux straits, the Poor Knights Islands and Motunau Island off Canterbury. Before the arrival of the Pacific rat, fairy prions also bred in many inland South Island areas, but a tiny relict population on cliffs near Dunedin is now the only known mainland colony.

One of the largest breeding colonies of fairy prions in New Zealand is found on Stephens Island, which is also home to the most significant population of tuatara. The presence of seabirds is a key factor in tuatara distribution; prions provide the tuatara with ready-made burrows, and their rich droppings support an abundance of invertebrate life. Stephens Island tuatara eat more than a quarter of prion eggs and chicks each year, but this predation seems to have little impact on the prion population. Although Stephens Island is a highly modified environment, fairy prions burrow in the grassland there and thrive because of the absence of rats, to which they are particularly vulnerable.

In summer, fairy prions range through temperate waters around the coast, in the Tasman Sea and east to the South Pacific. During January to March, dazed juveniles that have recently left their burrows sometimes turn up near lights in coastal towns. In winter, fairy prions are concentrated in Cook and Foveaux straits, around Taranaki, east of Northland and around the Chatham Islands, and occasionally wander north to subtropical waters off the Kermadecs.

🕊 *While the Australasian region has the greatest number of shag species in the world, by far the largest concentrations occur in food-rich cool temperate and subantarctic regions such as New Zealand.*

SPOTTED SHAG
Parekareka *Stictocarbo punctatus*

During their breeding season spotted shags are one of New Zealand's most colourful and spectacular native birds. They have foppish black crests on their foreheads and crowns, turquoise to lime green facial skin, pale blue eye-rings, and orange-yellow to pinkish feet.

The feathers on their wings and back are a fawnish grey, with a small, neat, black spot on the tip of each feather, giving them the spotted appearance for which they are named. In the breeding season they sport a distinctive broad white stripe from each eye down the sides of the neck, and sparse white filoplumes adorn their otherwise black neck and thighs. Outside the breeding season they lose all their adornments, and are plain grey and black.

Spotted shags are an endemic marine shag found on all three main islands. They are locally common, with estimates of numbers nationwide varying from 10,000 to 50,000 pairs.

They favour coastal waters off rocky shores, including estuaries and harbours, and forage for small fish up to 15 kilometres offshore. They can dive for up to 70 seconds at a time, although they average 30 seconds a dive, usually resting on the surface for 10 to 15 seconds between dives. They nest in small scattered colonies on coastal cliffs and offshore rock stacks, and during the breeding season there is much local movement between feeding and nesting areas.

They are sparsely distributed in the North Island, mainly around Auckland and Wellington harbours. In the South Island they nest between Marlborough and Banks Peninsula and on the Otago–Catlins coast, with a few scattered colonies on Stewart Island and along the West Coast.

After breeding, most spotted shags remain within 200 kilometres of their breeding grounds. They form large winter flocks of up to 2000 birds, often flying in long lines between their feeding and roosting areas.

The Pitt Island shag is a closely related but distinctive Chatham Island variant of the spotted shag, with a small, localised population of 700 or so pairs.

🕊 *During its average lifespan of fifteen years, a bar-tailed godwit flies at least 385,000 kilometres, equivalent to a journey from Earth to the moon.*

BAR-TAILED GODWIT
Kuaka *Limosa lapponica*

Eastern bar-tailed godwits are New Zealand's most numerous and best-loved migratory wader, feeding in flocks of up to 10,000 birds at places such as Miranda on the Firth of Thames. They are among thirty-two of the eighty-six species of sandpiper-like birds in the *Charadriformes* group that spend their non-breeding season in New Zealand, during the southern summer.

Godwits undertake some of the longest direct migratory flights on record, flying from their breeding grounds in west Alaska on a non-stop 11,000 kilometre journey directly across the Pacific. They arrive here in late September in small flocks and leave in early April, making a lengthier return journey along the East Asian–Australasian flyway. Godwits that breed in Siberia and northern Scandinavia make slightly shorter journeys to Australia.

The different species of sandpiper-like waders have very varied beaks, each suited to a different feeding style. They range from the short, 1.7 centimetre bill of the little stint to the 20 centimetre, curved bill of the long-billed curlew. At 10.5 centimetres — slightly longer in the larger female — the godwit's slender upturned bill is in the middle of the range. It is used for probing rapidly into deep sand and mud in search of aquatic worms and molluscs. Towards its tip the bill is richly endowed with touch-sensitive particles called Herbst's corpuscles that help detect telltale pressure changes made by buried prey. The tip of the bill can also move slightly, allowing the bird to manipulate prey underground.

During the northern hemisphere summer, godwits don't probe for food as beneath the wet surface the ground is permafrost. Instead, they feed on two-winged flies such as craneflies that are present in enormous numbers. The Arctic tundra provides ideal breeding conditions for waders, but the northern summer is very short so the birds must be able to migrate to less productive non-breeding grounds.

About two thirds of the godwits stay in the North Island, while the remaining birds are distributed around the South Island, especially Farewell Spit, the Marlborough Sounds and Southland estuaries. They spread out over sand and mudflats to feed at low tide, and as the tide comes in concentrate in large roosting flocks on high shell-banks.

More than a hundred Campbell Island teal have recently been released back on the main Campbell Island. These birds all descend from a single female, Daisy, who was part of a group of teal collected from Dent Island in 1984.

CAMPBELL ISLAND TEAL
Anas nesiotis

The flightless Campbell Island teal is the world's smallest dabbling duck, and is one fifth smaller than its close subantarctic relative, the Auckland Island teal. Both teal evolved independently, from two separate colonisations by New Zealand's brown teal, possibly as long ago as fifty thousand years before the last glaciation, fifteen to twenty thousand years ago. This is exceptional as very few ducks have colonised and survived on cold, glaciated islands.

Campbell Island teal is the darkest brown of the three teals, with the male having the most conspicuous metallic green colouring on its head. For the past 150 years the Campbell Island teal population has probably comprised no more than 25 breeding pairs, confined to tiny Dent Island by the presence of cats and Norway rats on the main island. They had been considered extinct, until a single female was briefly captured when a Wildlife Service party spent two hours on Dent in 1975. Tussock-covered Dent Island is 200 metres high, measuring only 650 metres by 450 metres, and the teal favour only the sheltered south and southeast slopes, hiding in a couple of moist gullies and on vegetated slopes below 100 metres altitude.

Burrowing seabirds cause high levels of soil disturbance, and their guano results in rich soils that are home to many invertebrates such as weevils and earthworms. These provide good food for the predominantly carnivorous teal, which also forage on the island's rocky shore. The megaherb *Stilbocarpa* also thrives in the rich soils, and the teal run around on the bare ground beneath the plant's large, umbrella-like leaves and hide in petrel burrows. Open, rocky spaces provide favoured roosting areas, where males sit and watch over their territory.

Campbell Island teal are very territorial and live in pairs. Their only displays are little comfort movements such as preening, which are appeasement rather than attention-seeking behaviours. Campbell Island teal lay clutches of three to four large eggs, with each egg weighing up to 16 percent of the female's weight.

Following the eradication of rats from Campbell Island in 2001, teal from Dent Island have been sighted there.

🕊 The yellow crest above the Fiordland crested penguin's eye is broad, and the tassel droops noticeably at the tip. Many birds have a characteristic white cheek stripe.

FIORDLAND CRESTED PENGUIN
Tawaki *Eudyptes pachyrhynchus*

Fiordland crested penguins are the most threatened of the crested penguin group, which comprises about six species, four of which are endemic to the New Zealand region. An estimated two and a half to three thousand pairs of Fiordland crested penguins nest on forested headlands and rocky shores in Fiordland and on the southwest coast of the South Island, with a few pairs breeding on Stewart Island and neighbouring Codfish Island.

Today, Fiordland crested penguins only occasionally stray as far north as Cook Strait, but fossil bones have been found in the north of the South Island and they probably occurred in the North Island as well. Fiordland crested penguins, along with yellow-eyed penguins, king shags and seals, were eaten by Maori, and today only relict populations of all these species survive in areas with low human populations. Weka and mustelids take many eggs and chicks, even quite large chicks in crèches.

Fiordland crested penguins are not very gregarious, and seldom gather and loaf onshore as other penguins do. They nest out of sight of each other in small colonies, usually numbering about ten or so pairs. The nest is a shallow, lined scrape in a cave, or under a log or bank in the forest, and is often quite dark, possibly to hide the birds from sandflies.

The female lays two eggs, the first of which is 15 to 40 percent smaller than the second. Incubation begins once the second egg is laid, and this egg usually hatches first. Although the first egg does usually hatch, the much smaller chick seldom survives longer than ten days. This obligatory brood reduction may be because parents can only find enough food to raise a single chick. While the first egg is a form of insurance policy, it is not known why they persist in laying two eggs.

Male Fiordland crested penguins undertake the first incubation stint after the eggs are laid, then both parents take turns. The female feeds the surviving chick until it's three or four weeks old, when it is more mobile and able to join crèches while both parents feed. During the breeding season birds feed in continental shelf waters close to the colony. After remaining in the colony to moult, they disperse north in winter and remain at sea. They eat mainly squid.

The tassels of the Snares crested penguin are thin behind the eyes and exceptionally bushy at the tip. The species is also identifiable by a prominent patch of fleshy pink skin around the gape of the bill.

SNARES CRESTED PENGUIN
Pokotiwha *Eudyptes robustus*

Although they breed on only one island group, Snares crested penguins make up in numbers what they lack in distribution. About 27,000 pairs are found in more than a hundred dense breeding colonies on the larger islands in the remote, undisturbed Snares group. The birds gather in large groups, usually in clearings under the canopy of *Olearia* tree daisies that are bent and gnarled by the wind.

Snares crested penguins commonly roost on the horizontal branches, sometimes up to 2 metres above the ground. The inhabitation kills ground vegetation in the colony area, which re-establishes when birds move to a new site.

Like the Fiordland crested penguin (see page 196), the Snares crested female lays two eggs, the first of which is much smaller; the chick from this egg usually starves within a few days. Adults stay close to the colony at the end of the breeding season, and return to moult before dispersing north for the winter. Some immature birds, however, disperse and moult on southern mainland beaches in late summer or early autumn.

Penguins have a 'catastrophic' or complete moult, and replace their three layers of short, dense, waterproof feathers all at once. They gain weight to prepare for the moult, as they will stay ashore for up to six weeks without eating during this time, conserving energy by remaining still and sleeping. They are very vulnerable to disturbance during this period, especially by dogs and humans. During the moult birds are often mistakenly assumed to be sick, but the best course of action is to leave them alone.

All penguins are exceptional swimmers and divers, using their powerful flippers to 'fly' underwater, with their short tails and legs serving as rudders for steering. New Zealand is home to more than half of the world's penguin species, and it is the centre of crested penguin distribution, the six or so species of which make up nearly half of all penguins. Crested penguins are long-tailed, stout-billed birds, with long, bushy tassels or plumes sweeping back from just above the eye. Snares crested penguins are relatively short, squat birds, and their bills are deep, grooved and very robust, hence the species name *robustus*.

🕊 *Yellow-eyed penguins are the only penguins with yellow eyes, and the yellow plumage circling their eyes and head is also distinctive.*

YELLOW-EYED PENGUIN
Hoiho *Megadyptes antipodes*

The yellow-eyed penguin is the largest penguin breeding on mainland New Zealand. With fewer than 2000 pairs remaining, they are considered to be one of the world's rarest penguins, and are most closely related to crested penguins.

While other penguins nest in noisy colonies, yellow-eyed penguins prefer secluded nest sites. They prefer to nest in forest, scrub or thick tussock, inland from sandy beaches, with vegetation to shelter chicks and brooding adults from the hot sun. Outside the breeding season, birds sometimes socialise ashore in temporary groups. Yellow-eyed penguins regularly come ashore in the afternoon throughout the year on the southeast coast of the South Island from Banks Peninsula to Stewart Island. They also breed on Stewart Island and surrounding islands, and on the Auckland Islands and Campbell Island in the subantarctic. Fossils indicate that they also used to breed in the northern South Island, and prior to Polynesian settlement they probably also nested in the North Island.

In late September to early October, yellow-eyed penguins lay two pale blue-green eggs in a substantial nest bowl of tussock, grasses and flax, under vegetation to provide shelter and shade. Both parents take turns to incubate the eggs for about two days at a time, and brood the chicks for the first 25 days. While the parents are away feeding at sea, older chicks may make forays away from the nest but come running to meet a returning parent, which they recognise from its calls.

Yellow-eyed penguins have a high fledging rate, but the first few weeks at sea are a critical time for a young penguin and many die during this period. Young yellow-eyed penguins eat more squid and less fish than their parents, which feed mainly on fish such as red cod, yellow-eyed mullet and opal fish. They can dive to depths of more than 160 metres to catch fish on or near the sea floor.

Nesting yellow-eyed penguins are vulnerable to predation by ferrets, and trapping is carried out at some mainland colonies during the breeding season. They are also vulnerable to trampling by stock, and major efforts have been made to fence out stock and restore coastal forest and scrub to ensure the survival of breeding birds on the mainland.

Little blue penguins are the world's smallest penguin, with adult birds weighing just over a kilogram.

LITTLE BLUE PENGUIN
Korora *Eudyptula minor*

Little blue penguins, or little penguins, are the commonest penguins in New Zealand, breeding from Three Kings Islands in the north to Stewart Island and the Chathams, and around the entire mainland coast. They are the only penguin that breeds in the North Island. They also breed in South Australia and Tasmania, where they are known as fairy penguins.

They are no longer as common as they were in pre-European times, as clearance of coastal forest and predation by ferrets, rats, feral cats and dogs have caused their numbers to decline markedly in some areas. They remain abundant on offshore islands, especially in the Hauraki Gulf and Cook and Foveaux straits. On the mainland their strongholds are Banks and Otago peninsulas and remote coastal areas, especially the bases of high cliffs inaccessible to predators.

Little blue penguins usually nest near the shore in loose colonies, although nests have been recorded more than 500 metres inland and more than 300 metres above sea level on predator-free islands. Their nests may be in burrows, in sea caves or natural cavities, or under vegetation, driftwood and buildings. In a few seaside communities, such as Oamaru and Wellington, little blue penguins may nest under seaside cottages, and they are noisy neighbours. When they come ashore at night they make a wide range of calls, from cat-like mews to loud screams, and deep growls to trumpeting.

The nest chamber is often lined with sticks, seaweed and flotsam. Little blue penguins nest between July and December, laying two eggs and often raising two broods in a season.

Juveniles may disperse hundreds of kilometres, but adults are sedentary during the non-breeding season, and regularly come ashore after dusk to their old nesting area, leaving again at dawn each day. During winter storms they may shelter ashore in their old nesting burrow. Although they can dive to more than 60 metres, little blue penguins usually forage within 5 metres of the ocean surface on small fish, squid and octopus. They vary in colour across their geographic range. Northern birds are slate blue above, shading to light grey on the sides of their face, while birds south of Banks Peninsula are a uniform deep blue. There are distinct populations of white-flippered birds on Banks Peninsula and Motunau Island.

The supposed resemblance of the long red tail feathers to marlin spikes earned red-tailed tropicbirds the name 'bosunbird' among sailors.

RED-TAILED TROPICBIRD
Amokura *Phaethon rubricauda*

Tropicbirds are truly oceanic birds that can remain at sea almost indefinitely, scorning land except during breeding. They have fully waterproof silvery white plumage, sometimes tinged rosy pink, and two striking, long, flexible, red tail feathers that can be 40 centimetres long. The red tail feathers wear quickly and are constantly replaced, independently of the rest of the wedge-shaped tail.

Tropicbirds have small, weak legs, feet and pelvis, and are virtually helpless on land. They fly using rapid, continuous wing beats, and have large flight muscles and a deeply keeled breastbone.

Red-tailed tropicbirds are pan-tropical birds that extend into subtropical areas, preferring areas of clear water with temperatures between 24 and 30 degrees Celsius. Sparsely distributed in remote areas bereft of other seabirds, tropicbirds are characteristic of the tradewind zones of the central and west Pacific and southern Indian Oceans.

Tropicbirds feed on squid or flying fish by swooping, or diving with half-closed wings from a height of up to 50 metres. They can capture prey up to a fifth of their own body weight, and emerge at the surface after a dive holding their prey crosswise in their finely serrated bills.

Tropicbird courtship advertises the male, rather than a nest site. It is a complex aerial display involving up to twenty birds, flying in large gyrations up to 100 metres above the sea, making ritualised wing beats, stiff wing glides and upward and backward fluttering, combined with calls. Once a pair is formed there are no displays at the nest site.

Tropicbirds nest on oceanic islands, preferring cliff cavities which offer shade and an easy take-off, although they will also nest under boulders on slopes and even beneath vegetation. In New Zealand, red-tailed tropicbirds nest on the Kermadec Islands, and in summer after a tropical cyclone a few birds may be seen around northern New Zealand, usually off Northland or in the Hauraki Gulf.

The single egg is laid in a shallow scrape during December or January. Tropicbirds don't have a brood patch, and warmth reaches the egg through the adult's stomach feathers. The chick develops slowly, and is fed on mucous-covered food carried in the parents' crops or lower in the alimentary tract.

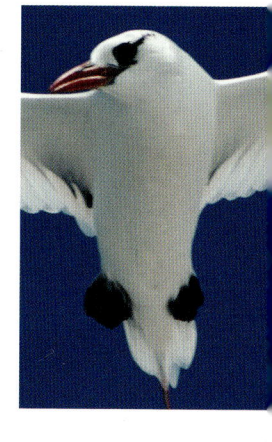

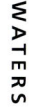

Wedge-tailed shearwaters accompany feeding dolphins and whales at sea, but don't follow boats.

WEDGE-TAILED SHEARWATER
Puffinus pacificus

Shearwaters get their name from flying so close to the sea on downswings that their wingtips often cut the water's surface. Wedge-tailed shearwaters are essentially tropical members of a large group of seabirds that is widespread in both hemispheres.

While the similar sooty and flesh-footed shearwaters migrate between hemispheres, wedge-tailed shearwaters are often more sedentary. In the New Zealand region they breed only at the Kermadec Islands, and migrate to the southeastern part of the North Pacific. Predation by cats and rats exterminated most wedge-tailed shearwaters from Norfolk Island and from the main Kermadec Island, except on a few headlands and coastal cliffs. Still numerous on the offshore Herald Islets, Macauley and Curtis islands, they should quickly recolonise the main island now that cats and rats have been eradicated.

Wedge-tailed shearwaters are fast-flying, and easily recognised by their distinctive long, wedged tails. More lightly built than other shearwaters that dive to greater depths, wedge-tailed shearwaters feed near the surface by shallow plunge-diving.

They breed in dense colonies alongside other petrel and shearwater species, especially black-winged petrels at the Kermadecs. Birds return to their colonies during October and clean out and remake their nests in November. The colony is virtually deserted during the first half of December while birds 'honeymoon' at sea, migrating to nearby feeding areas to gain weight prior to egg-laying. Wedge-tailed shearwaters are generally silent in the air above the colony, although occasionally circling birds make a wailing cry. They are very noisy on the ground, however. They come ashore from late afternoon, with numbers increasing towards dusk. The noise reaches a peak in the first couple of hours after dark, and again before dawn. Their call is a soft wailing moan: *ka-whoooo-ahh*.

Their single white egg is usually laid in a burrow, but sometimes under an overhanging rock or in a hollow log. In crowded colonies eggs may be laid on the ground. Both sexes incubate the egg for up to 54 days, and within days of hatching chicks are left unattended and fed intermittently for up to three months until they fledge. Although some yearlings visit colonies, most birds don't breed until they are at least four years old.

White-naped petrels are a subtropical species, inhabiting warmer waters than most other petrel and shearwater species.

WHITE-NAPED PETREL
Pterodroma cervicalis

White-naped petrels are large, slender gadfly petrels. They're handsome birds with a distinctive broad white collar and blackish cap. Their upper back is grey, with a prominent, dark, M-shaped pattern across their wings. Their legs and feet are pink, with black toes, and their stout, hooked bill is black with squat tubes.

Like all tube-nosed seabirds, white-naped petrels have well-developed nasal glands for extracting excess salt from their blood and extruding it from the nose. Petrels and shearwaters have tubes that are distinctively fused together on top of their bills. Gadfly petrels occur mainly in southern and tropical waters, and although their movements are not well known some, such as this species, migrate across the equator.

In flight, white-naped petrels swoop and soar above the ocean. They fish in waters deeper than 200 metres, for squid and fish which rise to the surface at night. They surface-dip or make shallow plunge-dives, using the extremely sharp edges of their strongly hooked upper bills to grasp and cut their slippery prey.

During the summer breeding season white-naped petrels range north and northeast of New Zealand as far as Fiji and Tonga, south to seas off East Cape and west into the north Tasman Sea. Between May and July they migrate to the north Pacific, feeding in waters southeast of Japan, and return in November to breed on Macauley Island in the Kermadec group.

White-naped petrels became extinct on Raoul Island in the Kermadecs in the early 1900s, and the breeding colony of 50,000 pairs on Macauley Island wasn't discovered until 1969. This population has recovered significantly since goats were eradicated, and the successful programme to eradicate introduced mammals from Raoul Island should eventually see the re-establishment of breeding colonies there.

White-naped petrels mate for life. Each breeding season pairs raise a single chick, caring for it for up to four months. Both parents share the long incubation period, alternating their shifts ashore with feeding trips that may last from ten days to several weeks. Occasionally, adults don't co-ordinate their changeovers and the egg may be left unattended for several days. Remarkably, petrel eggs have been known to survive up to six days of chilling to hatch successfully.

Gadfly petrels such as the Kermadec petrel are among the least known of the tube-nosed seabirds, because they are nocturnal, breed on remote islands and feed well offshore.

KERMADEC PETREL
Pterodroma neglecta

Kermadec petrels are medium-sized gadfly petrels, strong fliers with a wheeling, bounding flight that takes them high above the waves. They feed mainly at night, either sitting on the surface or dipping from the air to catch squid, small fish and a few crustaceans in subtropical waters.

Kermadec petrels have a wide range of plumage colours, from uniform brownish-black to ashy grey-brown with a nearly white head and underbody. They have a short, completely black bill. Their primary identifying feature is a whitish, triangular patch at the base of the primary feathers on the underside of the wing. These birds breed throughout the southwest Pacific, where they are now one of this region's rarest petrels. Of nearly 30 species of gadfly petrel found worldwide, 21 species are globally threatened.

In the New Zealand region they breed only at the Kermadec Islands and are mainly seen in the waters around these islands, although a few stragglers reach mainland New Zealand each year.

They were abundant on Raoul Island, the largest island in the Kermadec group, until the early twentieth century. Settlers diminished the large colony in the late 1880s and early 1890s by harvesting them as muttonbirds. Introduced cats killed adults and chicks, and Pacific and Norway rats ate eggs, so by about 1965 Kermadec petrels had all but disappeared from Raoul. Now that rats and cats have been eradicated from Raoul it is expected that Kermadec petrels will recolonise there. They continue to breed in good numbers on the nearby Herald Islets, with some also on Balls Pyramid near Lord Howe Island, and Phillip Island near Norfolk Island. They used to breed on Norfolk Island itself, but disappeared after human settlement.

Kermadec petrels are colonial breeders that nest on the ground, rather than in burrows like most other petrels. The female lays one egg in a shallow scrape under vegetation or in the open under trees. They can breed at any time of year, with chicks and eggs recorded in most months, although most birds return to the colony from August onwards and lay eggs between October and March. They are noisy in the air and on the ground around their colonies, making a loud, distinctive *yuck-ker-a-ooo-wuk-wuk-wuk*.

Masked boobies feed by plunging from high up into deep ocean, often chasing fish driven to the surface by tuna or dolphins.

TASMAN BOOBY
Sula tasmani

The Tasman booby is the largest of the group of masked boobies. They can have difficulty taking off because of their weight, so they usually locate their colonies on flat ground near cliffs that provide updrafts for easy take-off.

Tasman boobies look a lot like the closely related Australasian gannet, without the orange-yellow head, and the black masks on their faces give them a slightly diabolical look when seen close up. They are amongst the tamest of the boobies. While females make a deep, sonorous *kerk-kerk*, males have a whistling *pseep-pseep* call.

They are pan-tropical birds, breeding on oceanic islands adjacent to deep water in the Caribbean Sea and the Pacific, Indian and Atlantic oceans. In the New Zealand region 100 or so pairs breed only at the Kermadec Islands, mainly on Curtis Island. They are very rare vagrants to northern mainland New Zealand.

At the Kermadecs, Tasman boobies breed year-round, with peak egg-laying between August and November. Females prospect from the air and on foot to choose a mate and nest site. The two bluish eggs have a chalky white covering, and are incubated under their parents' feet, the webs of which are filled with warm blood vessels. Hatching eggs and newly hatched chicks are transferred to the upper surface of the webbed feet, so they don't get crushed.

The chicks hatch essentially naked but soon develop white down. Tasman boobies usually hatch their two chicks about five days apart, but the larger first chick usually kills or evicts its smaller sibling. If the first chick dies, however, the second chick often lives, showing the survival value of laying two eggs.

The Tasman booby chick is brooded for two weeks and then often left unguarded; this is a dangerous strategy in the hot tropical sun but both parents usually need to forage. To keep cool, unguarded chicks flutter their gular pouch and turn their back to the sun, cocking up their tails in an attempt to keep their head in their own shadow. Chicks leave the nest at four months and may return to breed when they are as young as two years old.

Grey ternlet chicks solicit for food by pecking at the webs of their parents' feet, rather than at their bills.

GREY TERNLET
Procelsterna cerulea

Grey ternlets are delicate blue-grey tropical terns, or noddies, often seen nesting on rugged sea cliffs, just above the reach of pounding waves.

Their flight is graceful, floating and unhurried. Feeding flocks of up to 5000 grey ternlets fly into the wind, hovering and fluttering over the water and repeatedly dipping down to pick up plankton and small fish from the surface. They sometimes skip on the surface like storm petrels, getting just their bill and feet wet. As individuals leave the feeding area they veer away to the side, circling around to rejoin the rear of the feeding flock and slowly working their way forward again. When feeding, birds usually stay within 20 kilometres of their breeding site.

Grey ternlets breed in the subtropical Pacific, including Lord Howe and Norfolk islands, as far north as Hawaii and east to the small islands off Chile. In the New Zealand region they breed on all the islands in the Kermadec group. They used to be thought of as vagrants to mainland New Zealand, until the summer of 1969–70 when many birds were seen in waters off eastern Northland and the Bay of Plenty. That year nearly 1000 birds nested on the Volkner Rocks off White Island, and they were also seen around Sugarloaf Rock in the Aldermans. Since then tiny groups, numbering no more than 50 pairs in total, have bred around the Three Kings, Poor Knights, Sugarloaf Rock, Mokohinaus, Cathedral Rocks and the Volkner Rocks.

About 3000 pairs of grey ternlets nest at the Kermadecs, and although numbers have declined on Raoul Island in the last three years, they should begin increasing again now that introduced rats and cats have been eradicated.

Grey ternlets lay their eggs between August and December, usually in cavities and crevices on cliff ledges, under clumps of vegetation and along cliff tops. However, they have also been known to nest in the shade of boulders along beaches and on bare, rocky surfaces out of the sun. Both sexes incubate the single egg for 32 days, and the chick is fed on regurgitated fish; this differs from other tern species, which feed their chicks whole fish.

TROPICAL WATERS

🕊 White terns have a fluttering and ethereal flight, and are inquisitive and tame. They will hover in front of an intruder's face, uttering strange twanging and wheezing sounds.

WHITE TERN
Gygis alba

White terns, or fairy terns as they are sometimes known, have exquisite snow-white plumage, and when viewed against the sun their wings are nearly translucent. They are beautiful birds with dark blue-black, slightly uplifted bills and black eye-rings.

White terns have remarkable nesting habits; they lay their single egg directly onto the bare branch of a tree, often scarcely wider than the egg and many metres above the ground. Occasionally they lay on a rock ridge, or even on a fern frond. Miraculously, despite sea breezes and awkward movements, they seldom dislodge their egg. Norfolk pines and pohutukawa trees are favoured nesting sites on Raoul Island in the Kermadec group; Norfolk pine branches are fringed with small, upstanding, scale-like leaves that act like a fence to hold the egg. Some eggs and chicks do perish during severe cyclones and gales, in which case a pair of white terns may re-lay if it is early in the season.

White terns are extremely rare in the New Zealand region, with just ten or so pairs breeding on Raoul, although the recent eradication of cats and rats may see a resurgence in numbers. The subspecies that breeds here also breeds in small numbers on Lord Howe Island, and in large numbers on Norfolk Island. The other five subspecies have a wide tropical distribution in the Atlantic, Indian and Pacific oceans.

From the first day after hatching the chick is fed whole fish, the parents returning from sea with two to five fish held horizontally in their bills. A week after hatching the chick is left on its own, clinging tenaciously to the tree bark with its sharp claws. For several months after fledging chicks feed with their parents during the day, returning to the nest tree to roost at night. Chicks not only need to learn prey types and foraging places from their parents, but they have to learn how to flutter near the water's surface to catch tiny fish without submerging themselves.

During the breeding season white terns are usually seen at sea within 100 kilometres of their breeding islands. Outside the breeding season they are more pelagic, and disappear from Raoul Island between April and August.

When roosting during the day, adult black noddies adopt a sunbathing posture, with their tails and one wing spread and their heads tilted to the side.

BLACK NODDY
Anous minutus

Black noddies have an ability unrivalled among terns to feed in surf around islands and headlands, nipping in and out of, and under and along, curling breakers with incredible agility. Unlike more temperate terns which feed by plunge-diving, noddies hunt by skimming and picking food such as small fish, jellyfish, plankton, cuttlefish and other molluscs from the surface of the sea.

Black noddies are medium-sized dusky tropical terns. Occasionally called white-capped noddies, they breed in closely packed colonies in tropical trees or, as on Macauley Island where there are no trees, on rocky ledges or in caves. Nests are built in the forks of tree branches, 1 to 10 metres above the ground. Their nests are shallow cups of soft leaves interwoven with seaweed, grass and tree roots, cemented with guano and sticky vegetable matter, which the noddies trample with their feet. On tropical islands where *Pisonia* trees are present, noddies use the sticky *Pisonia* fruit to bind their nest.

Nesting black noddies are very tame and easily approached. The single egg is incubated by both parents for 35 days. When the chick hatches it is covered in down, black on its body and white on its head.

Most adults leave the breeding colony at dawn to fish in the open sea and return just before dark. During the day, unattended chicks may wander away along branches, returning to the nest in the late afternoon for feeding. Once they are able to fly, young birds also leave the colony during the day, returning in the late afternoon or early evening to be fed by their parents.

Black noddies don't migrate, and during the non-breeding season they commonly roost on their nesting islands. They make a cackling *krik-rik-rik* call at their roosting sites, and colonies are sometimes so noisy they can be heard from 2 kilometres away at sea.

Black noddies breed widely in the tropical Pacific, from the Great Barrier Reef to Hawaii. About 11,000 pairs breed at the Kermadecs, on the Meyer Islets, Macauley, Curtis and Cheeseman islands, and L'Esperance Rock. They used to breed on Raoul Island, but were eliminated by rats and cats. Single birds occasionally appear around the North Island after northerly gales.

GLOSSARY

aquatic — living in or associated with water
arboreal — living in trees
avifauna — the birdlife of a region
barbs — the 'branches' of a feather that emerge from the central shaft
brood patch — an area on a bird's abdomen which loses most of its feathers and becomes engorged with blood vessels during the breeding season
brooding — sheltering chicks under the adult's chest
circumpolar — distributed around the Arctic or Antarctic regions
cloaca — the vent or common opening in birds through which the intestinal, urinary and reproductive tracts empty
colonial — living in colonies or large groups
cosmopolitan — complete or almost worldwide distribution
coverts — small feathers that cover the areas where the primary wing feathers and tail feathers attach to a bird's body
crèche — a group of young birds
crop — the thin-walled part of the alimentary tract that is used for the storage of food prior to digestion
cryptic — markings, colouration or behaviour to aid concealment
culmen — a ridge along the upper beak, running from the nostrils to the tip
dispersal — moving away, or spreading out
displaying — to make a particular display or posture at another bird
diurnal — active during the day
endemic — occurring naturally only within a confined area; unique to that area (see *native*)
euphausiid krill — small, abundant shrimp-like crustacea in the order *Euphausiacea*
filoplume — a hair-like feather with a vestige of barbs at the tip

fledging — when a chick has developed feathers and is able to fly or leave the nest
forearm — the lower part of a bird's wing, containing the ulna and radius bones
gape — the open mouth of a bird, especially a chick begging for food
generalist — able to live in a wide range of habitats, or eat a broad range of food
gizzard — an organ in the digestive system which helps grind food into small chunks
guano — bird excrement
guild — a group of unrelated species sharing the same lifestyle and feeding habits
gular pouch — a pouch of bare skin between the lower mandibles (the bottom parts of the bill)
hawking — catching prey such as flying insects while in flight
irruption — an unpredictable and sudden large-scale increase in the population of a species
keel — a ridge in the middle of the breastbone to which the flight muscles attach
lamellae — thin plates inside the bill, resembling the gills of a mushroom, used for filtering food
loral patch — a smudgy mascara-like patch around the eyes
mandible — the upper and lower parts of the beak
mast season — irregular mass flowering and seeding years, often of beech trees
migratory — migrating seasonally between locations
monogamous — forming pairs of one male and one female
nasal tube — a large tubular nostril on the top or side of upper beak
native — occurring naturally, but not confined to one area (see *endemic*)

New World — the Americas
nocturnal — active at night
nomadic — frequently on the move, not confined to one place
Old World — Europe, Asia and Africa
Palaearctic — one of the world's eight ecozones, extending across Europe, north Africa and north Asia, north of the tropics
palate — roof of the mouth
passerine — perching bird
pelagic — living in the open ocean
podocarp — a group of southern hemisphere evergreen conifer trees, bearing a pulpy fruit with one hard seed
polygamous — forming mating groups comprising one male with more than one female
primary feathers — the main flight feathers projecting along the outer edge of the wing (see *secondary feathers*)
relict — a population that survives only in a particular locality
secondary feathers — smaller flight feathers located closest to the body (see *primary feathers*)
sedentary — confined to one place
sexual dimorphism — significant physical differences between males and females in a species
shaft — the hollow spine of a feather
shanks — legs
speculum — an iridescent or bright patch of colour on the wings
stoop — a hunting technique in which a bird folds its wings and dives at its prey
taxonomy — the naming and study of the classification of living organisms
terrestrial — living on or associated with the land
vagrant — a rare visitor
vestigial — an organ which has lost its former function

More about New Zealand's beautiful birds

There are many books about New Zealand birds, ranging from identification guides to books about bird behaviour and ecology. The shelves of your local library are a good place to start, and new and second-hand bookshops stock many titles.

The Field Guide to the Birds of New Zealand, Barrie Heather and Hugh Robertson, illustrated by Derek Onley, Viking, 2005 (revised edition) — the standard guide.

Handbook of Australian, New Zealand and Antarctic Birds, Volumes 1–7, Oxford University Press, 1990–2006 — this substantial series is the authoritative reference work.

Field Guide to New Zealand Seabirds, Brian Parkinson, New Holland, 2000 — a useful identification guide to seabirds.

New Zealand Birds in Focus, Geoff Moon, Reed Books, 2005 — Geoff has spent a lifetime observing and photographing bird behaviour.

Wild South: Saving New Zealand's Endangered Birds, Hal Smith and Rod Morris, Random House New Zealand, 1995 — contains chapter-length stories on the fight to save our endangered birds.

Forest and Bird and *New Zealand Geographic* magazines also publish many articles on bird species, habitats and conservation issues.

Websites

The New Zealand Ornithological Society website hosts the latest checklist of New Zealand bird species, as well as giving details about membership, which includes subscription to their journal *Notornis* — www.osnz.org.nz

The New Zealand Department of Conservation website has fact sheets and species-recovery information for many threatened species — www.doc.govt.nz

The Royal Forest and Bird Protection Society website has membership details and information on conservation issues — www.forestandbird.org.nz

Index

Acanthisitta chloris 44–45
Alauda arvensis 92–93
Albatross 9, 158–167
   great 158, 159, 161, 163
   royal 158, 160–161
   wandering 158–159
Amokura 204–205
Anas platyrhynchos 132–133, 135
Anas nesiotis 194–195
Anas superciliosa 134–135
Anous minutus 218–219
Antarctica 149, 159, 171, 177
Anthornis melanura 15, 16–17
Antipodean wanderer *see*
   albatross, wandering
Antipodes Island parakeet 32–33
Antipodes Islands 31, 101, 159,
   163, 165, 169, 189
Anvers Island 171
Apteryx owenii 53, 54–55
Ardea novaehollandiae 142–143
Athene noctua 106–107
Auckland 131, 149, 151, 191
Auckland Islands 17, 31, 57, 63,
   101, 159, 161, 165, 169,
   171, 201
Auckland Island teal 194
Australian coot 152–153
   magpie 102–103
   robin 39
Australasian gannet 180–181, 213
   harrier 104–105
Aylesbury duck 133

Bali starling 77
Balls Pyramid 211
Banded rail 150–151
Banks Peninsula 191, 201, 203
Bar-tailed godwit 192–193
Bay of Islands 117
Bay of Plenty 215
Bellbird 16–17
Big South Cape Island 49, 57
Big (Stage) Island 49
Bird pox 81
Black-backed gull 176–177, 179
Blackbird 72–73
Black-browed mollymawk 163
Black-fronted tern 130–131
Black-necked pheasant 111
Black noddy 218–219
   robin 40–41, 75
   stilt 128–129
   swan 146–147
Black-winged stilt 129
   petrel 207
Blue chaffinch 91
   duck 136–137
Bobwhite quail 119, 120–121
Bollons Island 165
Booby, masked 212–213
Bounties Islands 166, 167
Bounty Platform 167
Bowdleria punctata 154–153
Brambling 91
Branta canadensis 138–139
Brown creeper 43
   kiwi 52–53
   quail 122–123
   skua 170–171
   teal 195
Buff weka *see* weka
Buller, Walter 10, 35
Bunting 93, 94–95, 96–97

Bush robin 75
   wren *see* wren

California quail 118–119, 121
Callaeas wilsoni 10, 11, 19, 24–25
Callipepla californica 118–119, 121
Campbell Island 9, 31, 85, 159, 161,
   163, 169, 171, 187, 194, 201
   teal 194–195
Campbell mollymawk 162–163
Canada goose 138–139
Canterbury 31, 35, 111, 131, 145,
   153, 179, 189
Cardueline finches 87, 89, 91, 99
Carduelis carduelis 9, 86–87, 89, 99
   chloris 88–89, 99
   flammea 98–99
Caspian tern 178–179
Cassowary 53
Catharacta skua 170–171
Cathedral Rocks 215
Catlins, the 191
Chaffinch 90–91
Charadriformes 57, 193
Charadrius frontalis 126–127
Chatham Islands 15, 23, 40, 47,
   57, 59, 75, 79, 101, 147, 151,
   161, 169, 170, 171, 173, 189, 203
Chatham Island bellbird 17
   kaka 23
   pigeon 22–23
   shag 172–173
   tui 15
   warbler 47, 79
Cheesman Island 219
Chrysococcyx lucidus 46–47, 79
Circus approximans 104–105
Cirl bunting 95, 96–97
Codfish Island 185, 187, 197
Coenocorypha pusilla 56–57
Colinus virginianus 119, 120–121
Cook Strait 131, 182, 189, 197, 203
Coot, Australian 152–153
Coprosma 33, 67
Cormorant 172, 173 *see also* shag
Coromandel, the 127
Cracticids 103
Crake 149
Cuckoo *see* long-tailed cuckoo,
   shining cuckoo
Curtis Island 207, 213, 219
Cyanoramphus malherbi 34–35
   novaezelandiae 30–31
   unicolor 32–33
Cygnus atratus 146–147
   olor 144–145

Dent Island 194, 195
Department of Conservation 35
Depot Island 167
Dieffenbach's rail 151
Diomedea epomophora 160–161
   exulans 158–159
Disappointment Island 165
Diving petrel 186–187
Dodo 22
Dominican gull *see*
   black-backed gull
Dotterel 127
Duck 132–137, 194–195
   Blue 136–137
   Campbell Island teal 194–195
   Grey 134–135
   Mallard 132–133

Torrent 137
Dunedin 63, 161, 189
Dunnock *see* hedge sparrow
Dusky seaside sparrow 95

East Coast 97, 121, 209
Ellesmere, Lake 139, 145, 147
Emberiza cirlus 95, 96–97
   citronella 94–95
Emu 53
English hawfinch 87
   robin 39, 73
Erect-crested penguin 167
Eudyptes pachyrhynchus 196–197, 199
   robustus 198–199
Eudyptula minor 202–203
Eurasian coot 153
European pheasant 115
   starling *see* starling
   wasps 17
Extinction 10, 11, 17, 21, 22, 23, 25,
   27, 29, 31, 49, 51, 53, 57, 63, 67, 69,
   75, 81, 95, 104, 123, 151, 155, 195
Eyles's harrier 21, 29, 63, 104

Fairy penguin *see* little blue
   penguin
   prion 188–189
   tern *see* white tern
Falcon 21, 31, 62–63, 107
Fantail 36–37, 42, 49, 109
Farewell Spit 193
Fernbird 154–153
Fiordland 29, 59, 63, 67, 69, 139,
   171, 185, 197
   crested penguin 196–197, 199
Forty Fours Island 161, 169
Foveaux Strait 189, 203
Fringilla coelebs 90–91
Fulica atra 152–153
Fulmar prion 162, 167

Gallinules 149, 153
Gallirallus australis 55, 58–59
   philippensis 150–151
Gannet, Australasian 180–181,
   213
German owl *see* little owl
Gerygone igata 47, 78–79
Giant eagle 29
   petrel 9, 168–169
Gibson's wanderer *see*
   wandering albatross
Gisborne 121
Godwit, bar-tailed 9, 192–193
Goldfinch 9, 86–87, 89, 99
Gondwana 53, 101
Goose, Canada 138–139
Great Barrier Island 151
Greenfinch 88–89, 99
Greenland 171
Great albatross 158, 159,
   161, 163
Great Barrier Reef 219
Grey duck 134–135
   fantail *see* fantail
   ternlet 214–215
   warbler 47, 78–79
Guineafowl, helmeted 116–117
Gull 174–177
   Black-backed 176–177, 179
   Red-billed 174–175, 176, 177
Gygis alba 216–217

Hakuwai 57
Harpagornis 63
Harrier, Australasian 104–105
    Eyle's 21, 29, 63, 104
Hart Creek 145
Hastings 103
Hauraki Gulf 203, 205
Hauroko, Lake 185
Hawden, the 35
Hawk 103, 107
Hawke's Bay 145
Hawk-owl 51
Hayes, Lake 153
Hedge sparrow 84–85
Helmeted guineafowl 116–117
Hen Island 49
Herald Islets 207, 211
Heron, white-faced 142–143
Heteralocha acutirostris 10–11
Hemiphaga chathamensis 22–23
Hihi 15, 18–19
Himantopus novaezelandiae 128–129
Hoiho 197, 200–201
Honeyeaters, New Zealand 15
    Australasian 17
Huia 10–11, 25, 49
Hurunui, the 35
Hutton's shearwater 65, 182–183
Hydroprogne caspia 178–179
Hymenolaimus malacorhynchos 136–137

Invercargill 101

Jackbirds 49
Jaeger *see* brown skua
Japan 209
Jeanette Marie Island 163

Kahu 104–105
Kaikoura Ranges 65, 183
Kaimohu Island 49, 67
Kaka 15, 26–27, 63
Kakapo 27, 28–29
Kakariki 30–31
Kaki 128–129
Kapiti Island 10, 19, 27, 39, 55
Karearea 21, 31, 62–63
Karoro 176–177
Kea 27, 64–65, 183
Kelp gull *see* black-backed gull
    hen *see* weka
Kereru 20–21, 23
Kermadec Islands 9, 31, 101, 189, 205, 207, 209, 211, 213, 215, 217, 219
    petrel 210–211
Khaki Campbell duck 133
Kidnappers, Cape 181
King Country 98
Kingfisher, forest 109
    sacred 108–109
Kiwi 9, 53
    brown 52–53
    great spotted 53
    little spotted 53, 54–55
Kokako 10, 11, 19, 24–25, 63
Kookaburra 109
Korimako 15, 16–17
Korora 202–203
Korure 184–185
Kotare 108–109
Kuka 20–21, 23

Kuaka (godwit) 192–193
Kuaka (diving petrel) 186–187
Kukupa 20–21, 23

Lapwing 100, 101
Larus dominicanus 176–177, 179
    novaehollandiae 174–175, 176, 177
Laughing owl 21, 31, 187
Lek mating system 29
L'Esperance Rock 219
Leucocarbo onslowi 172–173
Little Barrier Island 10, 19, 27, 79
Little blue penguin 202–203
Little Mangere Island 41
Little owl 106–107
Little spotted kiwi 53, 54–55
Long-tailed cuckoo 43
Lord Howe Island 31, 37, 47, 211, 215, 217
    boobook 51

Maori hen *see* weka
Macauley Island 31, 207, 209, 219
Mackenzie Basin 129
Macquarie Island 31, 189
Magpie, Australian 102–103
'Magpie, The' 103
Mallard duck 132–133
Manawatu 10
Mangere Island 31, 41
Manukau 127
Marlborough 31, 139, 191
    Sounds 173, 193
Masked lapwing *see* spur-winged plover
    owl 51
Mast seasons 29, 35, 43, 91, 221
Matata 154–153
Manx shearwater 183
Megadyptes antipodes 197, 200–201
Meleagris gallopavo 9, 114–115
Merton, Don 41
Meyer Islets 219
Milford Sound 81
Miranda, Firth of Thames 193
Moa 53, 55, 63, 65, 67
Mohua 42–43
Mokohinau Islands 215
Mokoia Island 19
Mollymawk 161–167
    Campbell 162–163
    Salvin's 166–167
    shy 165, 167
    Tasmanian 165
    White-capped 164–165
Monarch flycatcher 37
Mongolian pheasant 111
Morepork 50–51
Morus serrator 180–181, 213
Motunau Island 189, 203
Mottled petrel 184–185
Mute swan 144–145
Muttonbird 57, 183, 211

Napier 103
Nelson 59, 67, 111
Nestor meridionalis 15, 26–27
Nestor notabilis 27, 64–65
New Caledonia 31, 175
New Guinea 15, 39, 51, 81, 103, 109, 123, 135, 147, 153
New Zealand black-browed mollymawk *see* Campbell mollymawk
    Forest and Bird Protection Society 11
    pigeon 20–21, 23

quail 123
robin 38–39
snipe 56–57
thrush *see* piopio
Ngutu parore 126–127
Nightingale 73
Ninox novaeseelandiae 50–51
Norfolk Island 37, 47, 207, 211, 215, 217
Northland 45, 85, 117, 123, 127, 189, 205, 215
Notiomystis cincta 15, 18–19
Numida meleagris 116–117

Oamaru 203
Opotiki 59
Orange-fronted parakeet 34–35
Orbell, Dr Geoffrey 69
Ostrich 53
Otago 111, 133, 139, 153, 182, 191
    Peninsula 203
Owl, laughing 21, 31, 187
    little 106–107
    tropical 51
Oxpecker 77

Pachyptila turtur 188–189
Pacific Ocean 159, 205, 213, 217
Palaearctic 73, 85, 89, 95
Paradise shelduck 140–141
Parakeet 43
    Antipodes Island 32–33
    black-fronted 33
    orange-fronted 34–35
    red-crowned 30–31
    Reischek's 33
    Society Island 33
    yellow-crowned 31
Parasitism 43, 47
Parea 22–23
Parekareka 190–191
Passer domesticus 82–83
Peafowl 9, 112–113
Pegasus, Port 169
Pelecanoides urinatrix 186–187
Pelican 160
Penguin 31, 33, 167, 171, 196–203
    erect-crested 167
    Fiordland crested 196–197
    little blue 202–203
    Snares crested 198–199
    yellow-eyed 197, 200–201
Petrel 9, 63, 168–169, 184–187
    diving 186–187
    fulmarine 169
    gadfly 185, 209, 210, 211
    giant 9, 168–169
    Kermadec 210–211
    mottled 184–185
    white-naped 208–209
Petroica australis 38–39
    traversi 40–41
Phaethon rubricauda 204–205
Phasianus colchicus 9, 110–111
Pheasant 9, 110–111, 117
Philesturnus carunculatus 10, 11, 25, 42, 48–49
Phillip Island 211
Pigeon 20–23, 49
    Chatham Island 22–23
    New Zealand 20–21, 63
Piopio 75
Pipit 93
Pipiwharauroa 46–47, 79

Pitt Island 15, 40
Pitt Island shag 173, 191
Piwakawaka 36–37
Plover 100–101, 126, 127
    spur-winged 9, 100–101, 127
Pokotiwha 198–199
Poor Knights islands 17, 151, 189, 215
Porphyrio hochstetteri 63, 68–69
    melanotus 148–149
Poulter Valley 35
Prion 188–189
Procelsterna cerulean 214–215
Prosthemadera novaeseelandiae 9, 14–15
Prunella modularis 84–85
Pterodroma cervicalis 208–209
    inexpectata 184–185
    neglecta 210–211
Puffinus huttoni 65, 182–183
    pacificus 206–207
Pukeko 148–149, 153
Purple swamp hen 149
Putangitangi 140–141

Quail 56, 118–123
    bobwhite 119, 120–121, 123
    brown 122–123
    California 118–119, 121, 123
    New Zealand 123
    stubble 123
Queen Charlotte Sound 16

Rail, banded 150–151
    Dieffenbach's 151
    family 59, 69, 149, 151
Raoul Island 209, 211, 215, 217, 219
Red-billed gull 174–175, 176, 177
Red-crowned parakeet 30–31
Redpoll 98–99
Red-tailed tropicbird 204–205
Rhea 53
Rhipidura fuliginosa 36–37
Rifleman 44–45, 67
Ring-necked pheasant *see* pheasant
Riroriro 47, 78–79
Robin, New Zealand 38–39
    black 40–41, 75
    English 39, 73
Rock wren 45, 66–67
Ross Sea 163
Rotorua 117, 147, 179
Royal albatross 160–161
    spoonbill 153
Ruru 50–51

Sacred kingfisher 108–109
Saddleback 10, 11, 25, 42, 48–49
Salvin's mollymawk 166–167
Sandpiper 57
Scandinavia 89, 139, 193
Shag 172–173, 190–191
    Chatham Island 172–173
    king 173
    Pitt Island 173, 191
    spotted 190–191
    Stewart Island 173
Shearwater 169, 182–183, 206–209
    Hutton's 65, 182–183
    manx 183
    sooty 57
    wedge-tailed 206–207
Shelduck, paradise 140–141
Shining cuckoo 46–47, 79
Silvereye 15, 80–81, 109
Sisters, the 161, 169

Skua, brown 170–171
    south polar 171
Skylark 92–93
Snare Islands 57, 163, 167, 185, 189, 199
Snares crested penguin 198–199
Snipe, New Zealand 56–57
Solander Island 185
Solomon Islands 37, 47
Song thrush 73, 74–75
Sooty shearwater 57
South-East Asia 27, 43, 133, 153
South East Island 15, 41
South Georgian diving petrel 187
Southland 101, 133, 193
Sparrow 82–85
    hedge 84–85
    house 82–83
Spotted shag 190–191
Spur-winged plover 9, 100–101
Star Keys 173
Starling 9, 76–77
Stead's bush wren 49
Stephens Island 67, 189
Sterna albostriata 130–131
Stewart Island 25, 27, 29, 35, 39, 43, 49, 59, 169, 171, 185, 191, 197, 201, 203
    snipe 49, 57
Stictocarbo punctatus 190–191
Stilbocarpa 195
Stilt, black 128–129
    pied 129
Stitchbird 15, 18–19
Storm petrel 33, 158, 159
Strigops habroptilus 27, 28–29
Sturnus vulgaris 9, 76–77
Sugarloaf Rock 215
Sula tasmani 212–213
Swamp quail *see* brown quail
Swan Lake 144
Swan, black 146–147
    mute 144–145
Synoicus ypsilophorus 122–123

Taiaroa Head 161
Takahe 63, 68–69, 149
Takapu 180–181, 213
Taranaki 189
Taranui 178–179
Tarapunga 174–175
Tasman booby 212–213
Tasmania 37, 81, 147, 203
Tasmanian mollymawk 165
Tasman Sea 163, 189, 209
Tauhou 15, 80–81
Tawaki 196–197, 199
Tern 130–131, 177, 178–179, 216–219
    black-fronted 130–131
    black noddy 218–219
    Caspian 178–179
    white 216–217
    white-fronted 131, 177, 179
Ternlet, grey 214–215
Thalassarche impavida 162–163
    salvini 166–167
    steadi 164–165
Thames 127
Three Kings Islands 17, 187, 203, 215
Thrush *see* song thrush
Tieke   10, 11, 25, 42, 48–49
Timaru 121
Tiritiri Matangi Island 19
Titipounamu 44–45
Titi wainui 188–189

Todiramphus sancta 108–109
Tomtit 41
Tonga 209
Toroa 158,160–161
Torrent duck 137
Toutouwai 38–39
Toutouwai pango 40–41
Tropicbird, red-tailed 204–205
Tuatara 189
Tube-nosed seabirds 158, 159, 167, 169, 187, 209, 210
Tui 9, 14–15, 17, 103
Turdus merula 72–73
    philomelos 73, 74–75
Turkey 9, 114–115

Vanellus miles 9, 100–101
Virginia quail *see* bobwhite quail
Volkner Rocks 215

Waikato 17, 117, 139
Wairarapa 139
Wairoa 121
Wandering albatross 158–159
Wanganui 117
Warbler 47, 78–79, 155
    Australian 79
    Chatham Island 47, 79
    grey 47, 78–79
Wattlebird 10, 11, 19, 24, 25, 49
Waxeye *see* silvereye
Wedge-tailed shearwater 206–207
Weka 55, 58–59, 151, 197
Wellington 51, 63, 131, 191, 203
West Coast 43, 59, 64, 65, 67, 191
Whale bird *see* fairy prion
Whio 136–137
White-capped mollymawk 164–165
    noddy *see* black noddy
White-eye *see* silvereye
White-faced heron 142–143, 153
White-fronted tern 131, 177, 179
Whitehead 43, 49
White Island 7
White-naped petrel 208–209
White tern 216–217
Woodhen *see* weka
Woodpecker 10
Wood swallow 103
Wren 9, 44–45, 66–67
    bush 67
    long-billed 67
    Lyall's 67
    New Zealand 9, 45
    rock 45, 66–67
    stout-legged 67
Wrybill 126–127

Xenicus gilviventris 45, 66–67

Yellow-eyed penguin 197, 200–201
Yellowhammer 94–95, 97
Yellowhead 42–43, 75

Zosterops lateralis 15, 80–81

North Cape
PACIFIC OCEAN
N
Bay of Islands
Poor Knights Is.
NORTHLAND
Mokohinau Island
Little Barrier Island
Great Barrier Island
Kaipara Harbour
Hauraki Gulf
Coromandel Peninsula
Muriwai Beach
AUCKLAND
Firth of Thames
Miranda
White Island
WAIKATO
Bay of Plenty
East Cape
Mokoia Island
Rotorua Lakes
TASMAN SEA
Pureora Forest
Whirinaki Forest
EAST COAST
Lake Taupo
North Taranaki Bight
HAWKE'S BAY
TARANAKI
Hawke Bay
South Taranaki Bight
Cape Kidnappers
Kapiti Island
WAIRARAPA
WELLINGTON
Cook Strait